Table of Contents

Preface 5

Self-Start.......................... 7
Journal.............................. 37

Self-Preservation 41
Journal.. 56

Self-Service 60
Journal 77

Self-Guidance.. 81
Journal.. 91

Self-Disturbance... 94
Journal... 119

Discrepancies 123
Journal... 145

Self-Abundance 149
Journal... 166

Self-Sacrifice 169
Journal... 185

Self-Redefining 189
Journal... 207

Self-Love 211
Journal... 226

PREFACE

This book isn't just for women. It isn't just for men; it's for all who seek better and have the urge to want better. Not for others' sake through which they feel an obligation to own, but for self-worth and self-growth. The matter of age doesn't amount to growth, as it is entitled its own. It is, in fact, the value of development; to each its own. My book is in the genre of confidence and self-positivity. To help improve self-esteem.

CHAPTER 1
SELF-START

"You want to open yourself up and take the leap that you've always wanted to take. To apply energy towards the vision grown within your person and apply it to the life you wish to not one day live, but to create. It takes self-growth and overall self-start from you and those around you to uplift and continuously motivate. Be the example you know that no one other than your physical well-being can take from you. To want it and go for it, how will you do it? And which direction will you choose?"

-INicole Royce

When simplifying self-start, it all begins and ends with you. So, here is where I brighten your horizon and draw your attention to the uplifted motivation of the phrase. The name self-start pretty much explains the meaning of what it holds, without too much overthinking behind it. But it includes more self-initiative, so to say, when it comes to what it truly stands for in my eyes, as I'm sure it will stand out in yours.

Do you find yourself wanting to start something; but remain calm? And do you go about having all these brilliant ideas with an overload waiting to flourish? I love the meaning behind the words self-start. Because I look at these word as power words within this book, "The Book of Self." It is more like the brainpower of all the other characteristics you will need, and all the others will soon follow. So when I think of the words self-start, I think of a starter kit. The kind of things needed to help build up to one's true self.

You want to be someone who can undertake anything without holding back, without hesitation. Someone who doesn't need an uplift or push to get something going, or the peer pressure of the thoughts of those around them. But someone who has self-motivation and takes the initiative to build the empire needed, to create the brand of something without being encouraged. That sense of encouragement someone can get due to thoughts of their own. There is a difference between doing something strictly because you feel obligated to, or because you feel that someone else's dream overrules yours and that yours is not good enough to be in the light. Another way is just being your creator and the mastermind behind what you truly stand for, and the creativeness you hold within yourself. If you had no clue of the exact meaning behind "self-start, "then the only real thing missing is you.

You will find yourself in the sense of still gaining overall sanity, without hesitation of losing yourself.

Your inner person has to offer so much that you never question it, and abide by doing so without hesitation. It's going to make you nervous when starting out, making it more and more challenging over time. The more you devote yourself, it comes to a point when the most difficult challenges become the easiest. I believe that with every self-start of someone there is something more powerful to

8

reach. We don't always notice these things, but trust and believe whatever you think will come true the sooner you give yourself genuine recognition for it. There should be a fine line between starting something for yourself and loving yourself.

I love to encourage those with these minds that we must never let it go to waste - everything is brilliant and to each its way; when I say this, I'm merely speaking for the upbringing, the mishaps, the good, bad, and the ugly. The beginning is where we will be soon, if we not have already discovered an overall experience. It is how we choose to come out of that experience and what it takes to get through it. There is no right or wrong way, but there are ways that are better than others. Although the way you choose to go in the route you decide to take is your business, there are positive steps throughout your self-start journey once you finally decide to take it.

There will be some people with a similar start, comparisons, or similarities, but nobody will ever be the same. No matter how many ideas there are, we all feel someone has ours within their thought process too. It's about how yours stands out and what makes your brand better than the next in its own creative way. It is that amount of confidence that you must build within yourself, to build yourself up. And there are many people out there who feel as if their one way is the only way. I'm here to tell you that it is not. It's okay to stand out and be different. That is one characteristic right there that will help you continue to shine and be you. I'm all about helping and guiding people who feel like they must be or do a specific thing to become uplifted and motivated.

The amount of confidence someone has gone a long way. It can determine many things, and be the reasoning behind why you either did or didn't do something. It falls in place of body language that stands behind not only you, but the actions that follow. I love to say that confidence will take you far once you've grasped the truth behind you and what you stand for, which is what we're trying to create within this book of self.

I believe self-confidence to be something that everyone can have, yet in their own way. You have multiple people who are themselves, and then you have those who feel they should be somebody else. And then you have others who interpret that same image of themselves, but yet ball their self-identity up due to a lack of self-confidence.

You have people who are perfectly comfortable in someone else's shoes and yet disappointed when it comes to the true them within their own four walls. That is when you have to sit back and genuinely think about the consequences behind your self-start. Don't prosper until things become too thin, or almost too delicate to dig ourselves up out of. People have accomplished some in the making or even in the bind trying to figure it all out.

The start-up of self and how you project determines the obstacles you lead yourself to go through. This is not necessarily saying that the person you are makes for the life you create. But, I believe it makes for the obstacles you have to go, through no matter the case, as you can form the life you wish to live by if you know what lifestyle consists of initially. Sometimes we know that we want something good, but we don't necessarily understand what. We know that we see what we see, think about what we believe, and want what we want. We need to be mindful of the energy that we deliver within ourselves. Because everything holds a consequence, which is an outcome of every situation we go through; it carries weight. Whether light or heavy, can you handle the result of your actions. You should try giving yourself peace of mind by being you if you haven't been doing this already, and restarting your self-start.

The self-start that you've projected and your interpretation in the eyes of others will be different. You'll be off-balance and continue to be off-balance the longer it takes for you to adjust to the real you. Not the you that makes you comfortable on the outside looking in. But the you that allows you to be comfortable inside looking out. You want to look at yourself on the inside with the same amount of confidence as you do for those around you. You can see within you the direction that you don't want to be heading in, and you should focus on not looking back or being continuously dragged into the direction you were going.

How many times have you considered yourself to have experienced a self-start? Like many people, we have multiple startups, so that's perfectly normal. It's okay to have a fresh start. You want to be happy within yourself, turn a circle, and notice that it may be no bigger than just a small process. And that it can be ok to backtrack and lose sight of your sense of direction sometimes. To figure yourself out, is how I look at it. There is no timing for when you'll figure yourself out, but it's the process behind taking the accountability to do that stands out most.

The average person will look at a self-start as how you start up your life at the beginning. That's not possible, no matter how deep you are into life, no matter the number of years. The self-start has a lot to do with the mental state rather than physically being where you are. There are different lineups in which I believe pertain to self-start, in which you'll always be starting up a new challenge, but as long as it's benefiting you in the long term then it's beneficial. The steps within your headspace allow you to face challenges no matter what environment you're in, given your ability to separate the two.

And in some cases, you're in the wrong environment. That places a huge role in the thoughts that you're able to gain, so try your best to find a space, if not places that you're able to go, which will help allow you to elevate your thinking into a more creative state of mind. I love to push people around me to dig deeper into their thoughts than just the idea that we have about ourselves or something abided by someone's normality.

"Don't look for it; continue to do what you plan as planned, and the pieces will fall accordingly. Otherwise, they'll drop, and you'll find yourself having to pick them

up continuously. When handled accordingly, you'll no-tice they'll begin to pick up themselves, and their place-ments will come naturally. Anything forced isn't a good fit for the perfect fit."

-INicole Royce

You'll soon figure out the start of what makes you the person you see yourself to be. Not by just looking in the mirror, but by getting within the core of you that you've not dared to reach. I'm all about getting things out of people they don't even see within themselves. I know how people judge themselves as those around them like to indulge. But, sometimes, you have to dig deeper than deep and go outside of the normalization, outside of your comfort zone, to find extreme comfort in things.

At times we don't want to believe this is true, but who we have around us can sometimes lead us in the direction of discomfort. Some things that we'd typically realize or notice won't allow themselves to fully prosper or direct you in the path you need to go if you're surrounded by the wrong people. I believe that timing is everything, and situations happen to us once we realize what we're missing. Things have either gone wrong by changing up our routine or possibly even eliminating things that took hold of our energy, that probably shouldn't in the first place. So whatever you decide to do, be mindful, and stay aware of your feelings internally and externally.

Don't move too fast, but time will only go as slow or fast as you allow it to. You will learn to tap into the inner senses, and you have to gain that discipline you're looking to have. It could all be so simple; it's okay to be dismissive. Not everything or is everyone good for you. I feel as though we sometimes forget that we came into this world alone, yet feel as though some of us need everybody. Sometimes, everybody can cause you to go back to square one for even learning your true self.

Let's try to get to know ourselves once more, no matter how many times you've tried or even attempted to try, or better yet if you've brought up the thought but never accessed the physical for putting your words into action. Well, this is your perfect time to start. Think of it this way - you have nothing else to lose, and everything that you've either lost or that you're losing was never truly meant for you in the first place as better things are waiting to come, if only you allow for those doors to be opened.

So, with your thanks for yourself, give yourself the simple respect needed for doing just that. You'll realize that there's so much more out there. Maybe even things are already happening or have happened for someone else, but never underestimate yourself or find yourself trying to compare yourself to others because you won't win. I have a quote that I stand by when it comes to thinking on this level, and I quote:

"We all have deadlines; sometimes, it's not met to match our dedicated time frame. Instead of seeing that as a discouragement, look at it as the outcome means better timing in making it all and striving forward. Don't lose

hope - still keep that same dedication towards the finish line and filled with greatness, so it's nothing less than to come the confirmation is already affirmative!"
-INicole Royce

Know Yourself Truly

There's more to the meaning of "self-start," but it's essential to start it all by just being you. It would help if you tried with the start of it all by asking yourself:

- **"Who am I exactly?"**
- **"Do I even know who I truly am or my purpose?"**
- **"Have I ever honestly just sat back and tried to get the chance to know myself on a more personal level?"**

One should get to know themselves on levels that one understands, and not be so wrapped up in the stories others perceive you to be. But you wonder if you truly know yourself. These questions might take you for a loop, but you'll be surprised. Just because you know who you are at a given moment doesn't mean it's the real you. Suppose you haven't yet reached the total growth you wish to happen within yourself. You can know who you are for that moment in time, and for those years you've lived and are living. But what happens when you begin to grow?

Your mind becomes wiser than before. You then grow out of yourself. And that's okay, to grow up and out if it's for a turn in the right direction. There is one thing being yourself and another when it comes to knowing yourself fully. There are so many things that trigger our nerves. Things which give us setbacks that we can't even begin to think about how to get out of; let us not forget the situations that take many of us over the edge at times.

When you finally give yourself a break, you eventually realize that a problem wasn't even as serious as you made it out to be. All these inquiries seem uncertain when you deserve better within any and everything around you. I seek things within people who I could share a gift with. But I would want to be that perfect example of practicing what you preach. I had a set of role models who, in my eyes, couldn't tell me any different, and I envision being like them and better so that I can give back the way they did and be that positive example for others. There is not a day that goes by where we as people do not wish we could go back or possibly change some things around us, or do quite a few things differently.

Of course, some people's situations are more challenging than others, and for that, I agree. That's why the steps to self-start and the steps within this book overall will help guide you. To not only know, but also understand some things that you probably had, which just needed a little more clarification to assure you that you were on the right path towards that growth you're destined to accomplish.

All these inquires seem uncertain when you first think about them because we all like to think that we know ourselves. But if we truly knew ourselves, would you be reading this book right now? And have this mindset of uncertainty, needing confirmation? No, you would not, because you would have no reason for confirmation. I think we at the beginning, like natural human beings, have been molded to be so in denial of this question, and don't truly understand what it means to understand yourself.

There are so many things that keep people from expressing their minds and continuously wandering. Have you ever been that someone or met that person who has an idea, it is going somewhere, and then suddenly it stops and has you trying to figure out yourself? We all get indecisive and are not sure what is needed. But when you slow down and realize that patience takes time, time is a virtue. There is no limit on anything, and effortless is limitless, as I would like to say. There are so many things that go through our wandering minds every day.

There are so many things that we see daily. But we need to learn to have the discipline to endeavor to set our minds to something and stick to it. There is nothing to it but to do it. I am still learning and leading while finding my way. I have always felt that I had the perfect ideas, but never put my thoughts into action.

Unfortunately, I would have the vision and then sadly lose it and hop right on board to the next idea that I thought was an absolute success. When, in all reality, it probably would have been a real success. But you must fully devote and conquer that one thing before you jump over hills to the next. We, as people, love to challenge ourselves, but fail to miss the obstacles of baby steps. We all want to try and play the part but not work the piece. This could allow you to feel your inner emotion and voice that tells you that you're not alone in your thought process.

I like to set a motive for getting people involved in "self-start" – and this is learning yourself. It would be best if you took the time to know yourself and understand your destiny I had to work on the person I am now, rather than the future I wished to hold. It doesn't mean that I didn't believe that I would see the end. But you must live for your moment and be realistic with yourself, while accepting that you are a work in progress. And that anything worthwhile will work out in the long run. There were times where I would not be honest within myself. I was in my own way, causing myself to lose my balance. Until I found balance, which is now easier to maintain, no matter how rocky, situations can easily be more challenging. And I believe that it allows me to handle them based on the levels of discipline that I had to come to with time.

The first step of it all is admitting that you need to work on yourself. It is one thing to know and another voicing that you are a continuous work in progress. I believe that anyone comfortable voicing that there is no one else to blame besides themselves is at the perfect start and end to any success pathway. I do not know it all, but I know enough. I know just enough to help guide one to the track I'm on, and I hope the rest will soon follow.

Expect that any questions that have been placed either on hold or just sitting in the red will come to light, and you will be open and willing to hear more. I'm all for lending helping hands and lending ears because I have been that person and had that wandering mind. I like to tell people the pros and cons of self-start other than the obvious: it starts with you and only you. It takes place with your ability to either change a situation it. By saying that, I quote:

"Never will anyone be able to completely walk you out of the now if you don't know."
-INicole Royce

This means that you have to want the change. Someone could guide you all day long and thoroughly assist you with everything needed to ensure that you accomplish your utmost accomplishments. But there's a difference between the two. It's when you then ask yourself, "Did I truly want it because I wanted it, or did I want it because someone practically leads me to a way out of which they felt was a good act?" I used to believe that within myself that I could do anything.

Meanwhile, I was living a life feeling as if I could not do anything. To second-guess my ability but knowing what I am capable of was a challenge to fight independently. And I believe that although it is pretty different in everyone and every situation. In some cases, the same concepts that lead one to the water lead another somewhere else. So, although conditions are different, and some have stricter timescales than others, who can say that because the situations were challenging, you have it any more complicated?

You can achieve the same rules and steps to guidance within yourself. Of course, you have to believe within yourself that you have the same capabilities and the same willpower as anyone else. It's all in your mind, but of course, everyone's not programmed the same. All of this explains my reasonings as to why I wrote this book - to help reach out to those who have a tough time knowing where to start. But have an even more challenging time getting created yet have all the ideas in the world. I believe that everyone has an opinion. They need to apply it. Most people feel that their views are useless or are even afraid to speak about their ideas.

The reason for this is that our world is so viciously judgmental, but endless - one's vision is another man's treasure. I sure feel like my thoughts are and could very much be one's glory more than one. I used to be that person, to think that my words had no meaning. Yet, I would always write, and I would hear how it was full of such importance. That is backward, huh? Yeah, it is one thing to know that you have a gift of something yet see someone else doing the same thing, but second-guess yourself when the light is shining on you. We like to give credit for the sake of others who have done the same things we want to. But yet, we don't realize that they hold a story behind it. It's funny, quite amusing, better yet so that we give credit to those who've already made it.

Whether people believe it or not, ultimately, we're comfortable being in the same situation; because we feel like it's too hard or too late. Because of the way we think. The theory of what and where we believe we are entitled to be at a point in our lives.

Due to age and after that turning point, we say no to ourselves, "It's too late for me to do this or that." And then, leading ourselves to believe that it's so when in reality we're brainwashing ourselves and manipulating our intelligence, belittling ourselves as a whole in what we possibly stand for and the gift that we each can excel. And to be honest, we trick ourselves into believing that our possible time for success has a time limit. There is no time limit on success.

Although time is not forever, it is, for the most part, what you make of it. Did you know that time isn't forever? It goes much slower when you're not making anything of it to occupy your time on a successful level, in comparison to someone valuing the importance of that time as you should. Well, guess what, you should, and that same someone could indeed be you! You can believe that everything you see is entitled to you as much as it is to another, so go for it! We're so blissful when it comes to supporting old money or those who've built an empire off of financial fame or even another one's name, and we don't take the initial credit to do so in the most positive ways that we know how from the ground up.

As extraordinary people, we fail to apply praise and believe in ourselves. We try and take the easy way of thinking we cannot be the initial mastermind. I have come to an even more profound realization myself and have not only realized for myself but, most importantly, my self-start, and where it all begins and how we can all seek the end. There are times where you must keep hitting that wall even when it means that the fence is continuing to build itself right back up, even when you think it's complete.

There will always be a wall that comes up in life as you try to overcome the challenges that dare to come your way. To continuously make its presence seen, without you knowing whether or not it's too much to handle. I was always strong, risk-taking, still nostalgic, dedicated, but never true to myself throughout life. I've always put the fundamentals of having all those characteristics to pursue others' dreams.

I would assure them that they had what was needed of them to achieve and at least be on the right track. But never would I feed into my guidance or, better yet, the excellent advice that I was by far the most ideal. There were always things told to me that I still never really got through my head until now.

At 27 years of age, I continue to look back and take from previous lessons. I like to talk about the meaning behind self-start. I know that it's most important always to put yourself first and start with yourself. No, it is not selfish, nor is it the wrong thing to do when you put yourself before others.

If only people would apply the same energy amongst themselves and believe that they contain just as much self-worthiness as the next. Then, in that case, our world would be off to a much better start. But, there's no need for complaining. Everyone has their way and there are the ways of many to handle. There is a start and finish to every situation given. And it just takes the right spirit to want to do so.

The Steps to Self-Start
Steps to self-start include motivations such as:

- **Assuring yourself that you believe in yourself, that you'll never second-guess your judgment.**
- **Listening and always keeping your eyes and ears open; give no one else any lead to think differently.**
- **It would be best if you moved differently to get different results.**

You must never forget that not everyone has your best interests at heart. You must understand that if you're already at the bottom after being hit so low and feeling there's nothing you're able to do, you still have everything in the world to accomplish. If only you put your mind to it and get to it. Yet everything seems to take so long to fulfill it's like you end up grasping your thoughts. You write it down.

To be entirely realistic, you may even speak about it or even let it simmer and just all play out into its pure effect. Because maybe you feel as though talking on it gets you nowhere, or letting it be complacent gets you nowhere. When in all reality, it's neither of that when it's genuinely all within you. You have to seek the outcome of your opportunities. It takes you to change your original habits. It takes you to do something different than what you are used to doing. It takes you to let go and grab hold of things different from what you'd typically do or people whom you'd place yourself around—all while thinking that their energy in the path or overall intentions were the same as yours.

Sometimes you must let go of the things you felt were forever. Some things are only temporary forevers, whether we want to accept that as humans or not - we're at times in such disbelief that those closest to us don't have our best intentions. Those closest to us are at times our worst enemies or even in some cases, what may be the cause of holding you back from prospering yourself into becoming.

It's for the better once you realize that you don't need a circle of people around you who don't seek the same intentions you desire for yourself. You need to focus on what you desire - whether it's a career, a life goal you'd like to complete, or even something you want years from now.

You can't hope and wish for the stars if you're not willing to place yourself around them. It will help if you become one with anything that you seek to be. I believe that this is essential, even if that means sacrificing something. To make a sacrifice is not the most comfortable of situations. But most importantly, it allows a person to grow - the moment you accept the fact that you must sacrifice.

The, the sooner you become your true destiny. The more significant in yourself and for those around you who I'm pretty sure you wish you could help. And for those of who you want to, you can better reach out. Meanwhile, you are at a conscious halt in life and battle with yourself about where you are not in the midst of where you're trying to get.

Who are you genuinely becoming, and who would you like to be?

Yes, you say you're you, and you know who you are. Yet, every day that surpasses you, means you then start to question yourself again and have doubt. So, do you truly know who you are becoming if you have not indeed become just that? Do you truly know who you are? I truly believe everything I'm pointing out to you is the endless questions I ask myself daily. That's what makes this book that I'm writing crucial on so many levels; because I'm speaking on a day-to-day basis. Every time I succeed and move another step forward, I'm taking it all in and jotting down my notes. And my notes are within this book - hopefully, to guide those in continuous belief while in disbelief while their adventures will never be over.

Meanwhile, you have hope at the same time that you're just in between your thoughts and can't get out of them as fast as you'd like, having to live through your situation of survival and still trying to maintain a daily life balance. It's only fitting to have doubts. It's only suitable to be confused. It's only right to let go of something, whether for the moment or ultimately. It's okay to let go!

It would help if you remembered that not everything has to have a downbeat ending or makes for a good ending.

There are quite a few things of pure uncertainty that you do not have the answers to, and for some, you may never truly have the answers because of their endless endings. To each its own, is what I say best fits. In some cases, you'll never have the answer to what you want to hear. At times, we might feel that sometimes we hold the response to certain things that are temporarily heard, but don't always mean that it's unentitled. Don't get discouraged. Just continue to use the milestones that you're going through to captivate and mold you into a healthier you in the process.

There's a step in everything, and you should begin admitting those life changes and going about them in the direction you know, which is upwards. Never go backwards and backtrack if that means leading you off track. Now, keep in mind after you've become disciplined about handling which situation you choose accordingly, you'll then be able to pick up where you left off, and going backward could work in your favor because that will allow you to close seeds planted. But that's a different chapter within itself and the direction headed in.

We as humans are capable of so much, and not even we as people genuinely understand our reasonings the way we'd like to understand them. Most of the challenges that we face are already created and molded to test us. But if we're not listening to our signs, we will never be able to catch them. And that's when sometimes it ends up being too late, which is why we need to get on the right path of mind first. And it starts within yourself. Don't leave yourself on the back burner trying to secure others' intentions and those around you. It's okay to limit yourself, limit your thoughts, disclose or not disclose information if that means protecting yourself. Each situation has an outcome, and everyone is different from each other. How one person may deal with something or someone may not always work with you. And I say that you should handle everyone and everything accordingly.

The messages I gave you redirected another sense of mind that you did not once think you had. It could even be a mind that you do have that you weren't aware of. I hope that now you're able to get more in tune with that peace of mind and grow from it through each situation from here on out. It's okay to have questions, and it's okay to have uncertainty because it is normal. But don't allow "I don't know" as the answer behind a statement.

Because if you look, you'll find the answers. You're able to overcome whatever it is for you and those around you. It's the doors to greatness, and greatness is within you. Remember, you are of value, passion, and purity. You are of devotion and complete growth, overcoming your superpowers that you did not once think you had. But let this be the one time of many and the final time that you make that genuine promise to yourself that you'll put yourself first. Know that you've made it and are continuously making it. It's easier said than done, but while saying it, your words are doing the actions.

Therefore, it's because you're speaking everything into existence. It's up to you to find that form and abide by it. You've made it and are continuously making it. Suppose you're taking the time even to read this book. Then, consider yourself made and appreciated for taking the steps towards yourself that you're taking. If you're not already focused, or better yet, if the thought of putting yourself before anything else hasn't been the question of concern, it's time to change that; because without those thoughts, you wouldn't be reading this book either. So there you have it; we all win, and we're all winners!

The Understanding of It All

The meaning of self-start falls in the guidelines of many things. Not just as a person, but yourself by looking more profound than just deep in others' eyes. But also regarding what you think and how you feel. As humans, we are either quick to judge or have a confident expectation of something or someone without truly knowing what we abide by and truly stand for. But how we can pinpoint and keep up with the lives that we think we know when it comes to those amongst us, when we have no clue what we really want! I bet without a doubt in my mind that if it comes to someone knowing their self-start, how many would be able to share or willing to communicate without having to brainstorm, over-analyze, or over think it all without genuinely knowing the answer? I then ask myself, as you should also ask yourself: Am I upset at my well-being or about someone else? And why is urgency of looking into the foundations of everything in myself not a top priority?

Most likely, people are insecure need an outlet. It is difficult - to know who you are as a person, learn your task, create a goal, a mind-boggling journey. And grasp that adventure that you'll then begin to put into play and live the life you created. I always say that a person learns the fundamentals of self-start and how much control you'll then have after capturing your moment of truth into moments of self.

Now let's try asking yourself what lifelong jeopardy is without self-start. When a person must deal with long-life jeopardy, not knowing what you want or who you are, it's typically never good. That perhaps means whatever it is that you've tried to conquer or wish you concurred, you've lost it, or it's done harm to you. In other words, a symbolization of failure.

I believe that nobody is a failure, nor should you ever consider yourself to be such. If you're someone who hasn't experienced loss, then you're not learning. Anyone anxious to come out successfully and willing to learn and grow overall will not become discouraged from the word failure, because it doesn't mean you're a failure. When you're someone who keeps going while getting knocked down you're not a failure, but it might take one person more time than the next to reach that stage in life that they hope to surpass. All that has anything to do with self-start falls in place as it helps set the foundation where you seek yourself being.

Who is it to say that you can't completely turn your self-start around and end with an even better outcome than your beginnings? But once you start with yourself, you will begin to understand why the meaning is so impactful in correspondence with each and everything you meet, and why it always begins with you.

Whether you are the mind, the creator, or the originator, you have just as big of a role played from start to finish. The beginning of the race can have its glitches, but it's how you finish that counts. I like to give examples of self-start from my truth by writing this to those of you battling these same questions of minor setbacks. Let us stop pointing the finger all the time at why something is or ended up with the outcome that it ended up with that has placed you in the predicament that you're in at the moment. I believe that I and everyone else are capable of everything, and sometimes others' strength needs a little work.

I wouldn't want anyone to lose that quality. So I'm here to help you try and find it. When in doubt and you feel as though there aren't any ears besides your own, I hope to believe that you'll open this book as if you're speaking to someone who's speaking right back to you loud and clear. There is so much out there to know and explore. To help you try and find yourself within yourself! I have been that person and until this day, I still am that person.

The person who feels like she should have been way ahead of her time and a much better lifestyle than the one she's in currently. But beggars can be choosers, right? I've had practically everything that I could ever dream of having. And yet, I've always wanted to be able to share that same amount of energy that I've received. It's sometimes tiresome not being able to do or see something and realizing that you had the same opportunities. But it hits differently after discovering that it's the timing that could be all wrong.

I remember learning to tell myself that it might feel like the perfect moment, but that does not always mean the timing is your turn. After thinking, hoping, and dreaming, I beat myself up time after time and dream that I wanted better and could do better. When in doubt, you feel as though there aren't any ears but your own. I hope to believe that you'll open this book as if you're speaking to someone who is speaking right back to you loud and clear. To have a sense of belief that you're not only thinking what you're thinking or feeling the way you're feeling alone, or the only one to constantly feel as though you're mistaken or stuck.

To gain the belief and secure understanding of the first step, "self-start" will place you on the correct open path towards opportunity. I stress this entirely when I say put just as much recognition into yourself as to others and you'll begin to see more than what is on the platter laid out for you. You will begin to notice that once you follow your steps towards your happiness, you'll continuously grow within yourself without leaving yourself.

I believe that you can leave yourself behind while trying to find yourself and leave someone else behind while carrying such a huge load. The only difference is that you have to take yourself with you, because there's only one you. There is only one life and multiple tries at it, depending on how you live it. If you treat yourself with the proper care and persistence, you will go far. I believe that you will pick right back up where you once left off because the true you within will never indeed lose itself. I think that the true you within just never had that opportunity to show their true colors in the midst of being blindsided with everything around them, rather than focusing on the core. Which, to me, are the means that matters most.

Once a person allows themselves to go beyond and challenge their mind, they'll see that everything they'd ever believed in wanting is right there with them. And they don't have to go elsewhere to try and find it or be something they're not to try and live it. Because your mind, body, and soul know when they are being used and abused. They will only give what you put in, just as anything or anybody you may come across.

You get what you get, and you give what you shall receive. Now the question comes up, "Do we always want to accept or hear what we receive?" No, not all the time, but we should hear it out or take constructive criticism. As humans, we must believe in ourselves while working on ourselves. We need to understand that not everything has to be; even harmful things that may seem cynical or that generally make you upset or sad. Yes, we're human, so general things we adapt to, both good and bad. Unfortunately, some abuse the position by just running with it instead of being open to other meanings behind certain things, no matter the situation.

There must be a multi-way street, a two-way street, with everything in life. But I say multi because no matter how wrong or right someone thinks something is, whether it is a situation, something coincidental, an accident about something, or even something as simple as one's opinion, there are many ways of looking at it. I can without a doubt say that over the years as I've grown wiser within, not only with age but through experience.

I've learned that something is in my mind no matter how right I think I am. How much I can't entirely disagree with something that someone else says. No matter what, I always try to listen and take others' opinion for what they are. People become more open-minded to seeing things from different standpoints, beliefs, and a distinct sense of direction.

As people, we are quick to jump and justify something that we do not like because we see something based on our perception. But what makes yours suitable? And who says there isn't room out there for more than one way of seeing life? To only see things as a whole without always having a justification, or possibly even combining our thoughts so that we could create an empire together, instead of a war zone against one another. A village of separation with, "My idea is better than theirs, and what I say is what goes."

There is so much to self-start. There aren't enough words in the dictionary or enough action in our terms to explain and describe the different examples. But we all know and have the same type of experience regarding a few examples that I have spoken about within this chapter. I ask if you have thoroughly read and grasped the points that I have hit and addressed.

- **How do you feel about what I'm saying? Are you defiant?**
- **Are you angry?**
- **Do you find yourself calm and open to admitting that you have some faults?**

Do you feel like you're a know-it-all and no matter what, you don't see anything wrong with how you perceive things? And that you are entitled to only information you bring to the table? All of these thoughts continuously go through one's mind. And you could fall into this category of things that I have touched on specific topics. Are they wrong or right? It is endless, because I sure do not have anything negative to say regarding one's sense of thinking. It is not for me to judge. It is for you to be able to clarify and confirm within.

This book helps people talk to their inner selves and learn while building themselves; it's not for me to point the finger or be judgmental. It's for everyone to grow while at the same time realizing that your thoughts, experiences, the way you react and interact with people and to certain things, may not be wrong or right but perfectly normal. That's why I find it essential to talk about it, because not many people are open to fixing situations.

We need to not give up on those around us or talk down to them, but continue to push those who are keeping themselves down. There is a difference between pushing and force, and sometimes that difference takes a certain someone to touch an individual heart that maybe one person had already tried to grasp hold of, but did not have the outcome hoped for.

Whether verbal or physical, it's s known that everything in some way, shape, or form has an emotional attachment; its expressions are different. And sometimes, it is not always what you say, but who delivers the message to you. It is not still the closest to you that touch you. At times, those who surround you in maybe even the slightest second or even a stranger can touch you. I believe that messages come in all ways, shapes, and forms, and it is a matter of how and when we finally decide to listen. I've yet to start listening to how I needed to surpass throughout the years, and in continuing, I am still learning. It is pretty challenging, especially when it comes to realizing that you do not always have to have the last word and that sometimes listening is all the voice needed.

Meanwhile, silence yells the loudest cry at times. You wonder who is listening when there is nobody around at times. And yet, when there are those around, believe me, they're watching your every move. Whether it's okay, threatening, or indifferent, your action speaks volumes in the ways your messages are delivered. That's why I stand behind the meaning of self-start; that specific characteristic within itself is all that's needed to guide you to the track to take the following steps towards other traits that will continue to build you along with those around you.

Of course, those steps are self-preservation, self-service, self-guidance, self-disturbance, discrepancies, self-abundance, self-sacrifice, self-redefining, and finally, self-love. I choose these because I feel like all these topics are at the core of being at peace within yourself. Although there are others, these are just a couple of the characteristics that helped me build and continue developing my mind of the self.

I feel as though these are good starting points. And they will let you think and explore much deeper into your thoughts and overall finally challenge yourself if you haven't already, or possibly if you've always searched for that challenge that you had trouble seeking. So here is your chance to lay it all on the table. And if not all, then some, depending on how much you allow yourself to open. It will all be new and fresh at first sight, but very much needed.

I love helping people challenge their minds to reach places you felt you couldn't. In a loop, you feel it is difficult to escape. There is so much out there to know and explore. I never want anyone to lose that quality. I'm here to help you try and find it. When in doubt, you feel as though there aren't any ears besides your own. I am here to help you try and find yourself within yourself!

JOURNAL
SELF-START

BEFORE reading these chapters

1. "What is self-start, and what does it mean to you ?"

_____
_____
_____
_____
_____
_____

2. What value do you feel you bring to the world?

_____
_____
_____
_____
_____
_____

3. Do you feel as though you truly know who you are and/ or your purpose or character as a person?

_____
_____
_____
_____
_____

4. What are the core strengths of "self-start" to you?

_____

_____

_____

_____

5. What is your "why" to self-start and the meaning behind it?

_____

_____

_____

_____

_____

_____

AFTER reading the chapter

1. What's the meaning behind the question "What is self -
start?

_____

_____

_____

_____

_____

_____

2. What did you get from reading this chapter?

_____

_____

_____

_____

_____

_____

3, Now that you have read this chapter and got a clear understanding, perhaps. Now, Who are you?

_____

_____

_____

_____

_____

4. After reading this chapter, do you now look at who you are the same as before reading this book or differently? And is your purpose still the same as before?

_____

_____

_____

_____

_____

_____

5. Which 3 words describe self-start in your vision after reading the chapter compared to your thought before reading?

_____

_____

_____

_____

_____

_____

CHAPTER 2
SELF-PRESERVATION

"To preserve something valuable, such as yourself. You have a heart of gold. A mind filled with wisdom and the overall accomplishments of the many; you're either accomplishing little to none. You're too hard on yourself when you shouldn't be, yet it's okay to be consistent - have dedication, but preserve yourself and your well-being. To keep yourself intact, don't overdo what you're unable to reach that given moment and then stop because you think you're shooting towards the impossible. Allow time to run its course and preserve yourself. You are needed, you are important, you are amazing!"

-INicole Royce

To self-preserve is the key to your willpower and access to your heart, the abundance of knowing your true self. And the definition you as a person stand for to define your well-being. As a person and someone of self, you must be entirely in tune within and allow yourself to trust yourself as you rely on others. To have total gain and overall ownership of your mutual feelings, no matter how good or bad you may feel, and to own that feeling and abide by making it better before it gets worse. And you know how to turn around the tough when it gets going, because it will not be the last time.

In the Now of Knowing

- **What do you think of when you hear the word self-preservation?**
- **What exactly does self-preservation mean to you?**
- **Do you consider yourself to be a person who's self-preserving?**

To begin with the basics, you first have to ask yourself what the meaning of self-preservation is. The word preservation means to preserve something, meaning to save or the safe keepings for holding something, whether it is a person, place, or thing. If you then add the word self-preservation with that meaning, it is to prevent something happening to the self. In other words, to protect the self.

I love the thought behind the words self-preservation because not many of us use that phrase, but we're very dedicated in the act when it comes to protecting what's ours. Most of all, what's right overall and what we as people stand for when it comes to whatever the argument is behind it. The word argument doesn't necessarily have to be argumentative and mean something terrible. It could only mean having a disagreement about one thing over another. or something in dispute to what one is saying over another.

How often do we find ourselves in situations we feel we could have avoided? After misinterpretations of things, if only you or the other person or many persons involved had just taken a deep breath at the time, sat back, and analyzed. Yet, maybe it could've been relayed from one person to another via voicemail, letter, whichever form of deliverance.

Of course, I like to include the word self because this book abides by the self. It takes by "you" because you are the reflection of yourself. I want to put everything into a self-stand point so that you can see the review of how every one of these characteristics has control within you, and you're the guidance behind the meaning. And how you consume this information will say everything that it needs to say, all in action within you. I don't think that we sometimes break things down the way that we could, the way that we should, and how we would if we didn't have such high horses when it comes to taking accountability. I speak for myself throughout every circumstance too, because I am still learning. So why not place it out on the table for others to explore and think right along with me?

Mirror Yourself While Envisioned In Others

As we all know, certain situations determine the outcome of you. By that, what you say and how you say it could mean the same, but both may have two completely different results. I have become fond of situations such as one person saying something that someone else says the in other cases, yet with the same meaning. It is all in a matter of your delivery. At times, we as people are so stubborn that we won't change our ways. And we don't realize that sometimes allowing ourselves to step outside the box and do things that wouldn't necessarily make us who we feel we're entitled to be could have a much better outcome, because entitlement is the problem in most cases. It doesn't mean that you have to say yes to everything, but chooses these battles wisely.

Before acting on something, don't force or project something in the same sense as you'd project to someone else and expect the same result. If you investigate growth and maintain growth levels needed, learn to pick which circumstances rely on your energy. Sometimes, saying no is enough in most cases and being done with it. And in some cases, you feel you want to be of help, and the person is just not listening, or possibly you have an idea yet somebody else wants to compromise.

I like to break things down into self-understood, meaning that I allow myself to see things as well as those around me. Because I've come across many lessons that lead me to believe that at most times, that is the best way to understanding. For those who've heard the word preserve quite a bit, I use this because we use the word a lot - but do you look into the meaning of the story, or do you use it the way that you know how?

To preserve something we know is to maintain something to keep it protected in the best way possible at its natural state, the form you found it in, allowing it to remain well-taken-care-of. In other words, to preserve is to keep something in holding, in which this case is self-preserve, leading being the title self-preservation. It all plays a role and goes hand in hand when working on yourself. It will help preserve your sense of thinking and peace of mind in the best way possible. To learn what and what not to involve and revolve your energy around.

Find an equilateral balance in the best way possible within your mind, because you are what matters. I like people to understand that most of their outcomes determine their income. The way they intake certain things and receive particular items. The way you manage your mind state, and either allow it to build you or break you. When you are ten times ahead of your thought process over someone else's, you are then your own endurance.

Although situations can either make or break you, you are genuinely your own preservation at the end of the road and it's all a matter of how you value yourself and take care of yourself for the better, within yourself, and what you have to offer. So many of us do not plan to go down the paths we have been down, nor do we choose to run into continuous walls having continuous outbreaks to get a break. No, it is not what we choose; it is not the way we choose, and it is not the way you have to decide to stay. So I encourage everyone to continue uplifting themselves and be a continuous reminder that you do matter. You are somebody, so treat yourself as somebody as you make sure to treat others.

Meanwhile, losing yourself all in the mist brings yourself back to your sense of reality and finding not just a soul within, but your soul within yourself, that you either lost, are losing, or looking right at while looking straight through all in the same breath. I like to place this meaning of conduct behind the book of self - underlined with the importance of one of the essential characteristics we need to have and keep. To know when and when not to, along with how so and how come. Sometimes we un- derestimate the similar characteristics that we hold for something good. We insert the self into a placement in our everyday life without working it all in within our own life. Instead, we pretend to live a temporal reality that we think and believe in; it is just reality and non-surreal. Some- times, we're too quick to avoid completing our craft and mending the spaces. Life was already accustomed to liv- ing and filling the voids.

To become a better person and build up to betterment, instead of pointing the finger to blame, you have some parts of you that feel like you have to live a temporary life to mentally escape from the reality of the life that you're already living - because it's easier that way, right? To just put it all on the back burner for this moment in time. But, even when you feel that you've had enough and want for it to all be gone and disappear, the sooner we understand the faults, troubles, and trials that we have ongoing will not disappear, the better we will be.

Until someone in the physical wants to make that change happen, it won't; because we all know that it may be just a matter of being the one to do so for the better in everyone. I want everyone to understand and grasp that no matter what your life holds or what situations you under- take, whether you want to the same environment or be content with the change, you continue with the life you seek – even when you're on the right path, you'll always continue to contact with potholes.

The Lead to Follow

What is a leader if you are the runner? It is one thing to try, and there is another to be the one who seeks the attention to want something but never puts down the foot to do so. When I say that, I mean within ourselves and practicing what we preach, or maybe instilling things into others or dealing with certain things that we do every day. This book is "The Book of Self." I hope to meet my match within every single person who decides to read this, as I love to make everything clear. I will point out how to direct self-preservation to one of your ways towards growth within yourself, instead of everything outside of you or in connection to you.

We will work on our abstractions and understand the importance of dedication to that same energy within your person. I like to share my experience while writing about these different passages leading up to self-love and growth. I never truly understood that meaning of things that I surround myself with mentally, physically, and emotionally are so often the worth of someone else's understanding rather than your worth.

Meanwhile, make peace with and understand things around you about certain situations, yet continuously question yourself. Be sure and uncertain at the same time, whether you tell yourself something or deliver the messages to someone else. You then find yourself experiencing uncertainty. Everything you do or say becomes questionable, whether it's your questioning yourself or your actions questioning you, allowing you not to respond with complete surety but with questions. I love to say that phrase, "The way that you not only want to know, but know how."

We all have those moments we feel like we want something to go a specific type of course, but we feel as though it's not good enough, and we begin to fill our minds with a question, and those questions sometimes could either make or break you or better yet slow you down. The entire time you should listen to your know-how and go with the instinct that you know most likely never steers you wrong. Remember that one person's struggle is another person's success. If I have experienced it, then someone else out there has as well. And they are continuing to struggle and run from their problems of existence because of their irrational excuses.

The excuses of self-denial, uncertainty, not knowing, and the embarrassment of not being able to admit when so. I have been that person and until this day I am still learning how to become even better within myself and in the eyes of others. You will never truly be accepted no matter how much you pursue, but you will, without a doubt, be respected, even if that goes for someone not saying or ever confessing that respect.

You may not truly be accepted no matter how much you pursue, and no matter what, that's okay, but you will be respected, even if that goes for someone not saying or even confessing that respect."   *-INicole Royce*

No matter how much you learn in life and no matter how many people you grasp and think you have on a tightrope into the pure positivity of growth and prosperity, some will never give you that credit. And some will never give themselves the proper credit.

Give Credit That's Due To Self

Sometimes you know what you don't always want to believe, but what matters most is that you know. A person does not always have to voice something to see that they have mastered or accomplished something. When you can accept that you've done a good deed or even admitted that you had done not only everything possible, but also all in your power that you could do without destroying you as a person, then you're a winner. A person does not always need a thank you to know that they have succeeded.

Although, these gestures are friendly without a doubt. Everyone loves to hear how appreciated they are, and it's a beautiful feeling to get a thank you occasionally. What I'm saying is that you're not going to get that every time. And you will not get it while you're expecting it. To know who you are dealing with when it comes to people is a challenge. As humans, it can get quite frustrating and overwhelming. But should it make you any less of who you indeed are if it is from the heart of you, and with every bit of good intentions? Self-preservation goes miles and miles. It takes a lot of strength and more self-evaluation than anything else you could ever imagine going through when it comes to the way you see things.

Most importantly, how you see those around you. And bite your tongue over the battles that aren't worth fighting because, sometimes silence makes for the most noise! It's not about how loud you get or who you can easily snap on someone or something when something doesn't go in the direction you're seeking to go.

And when the time comes for those emotions to show, you'll know that everything you've done is all that you could do without destroying yourself. To find the balance within your sanity and ultimately realize that expressing yourself to get your point across doesn't always have to result from a negative tone.

Although that is always the first sign of aggression once someone has triggered you, we all get to that point because we're only human. But should that be the point that we allow ourselves to get to every single time we want to go across someone's head? No, it is not, but that's where self-preservation comes in. I have done a lot of thinking about how I used to be, and how I feel now is more conservative. There were times that I would say whatever came to my mind because I could and because I felt like it. I didn't understand the consequences of what was said or the hurt that I caused when I said I didn't care.

It's tough for you to realize that you've bothered someone else because of your hurt and entitlement to something, and that how you felt at the time was the only opinion that mattered. But when you take things in after going through the different challenges of running into other people, and different ways of thinking and doing something, you begin to pick and choose a little more wisely for what is more beneficial for your energy. To protect your life and withhold yourself and preserve your thoughts, your mind, your action to your chain of reaction, and realize that not everything needs a response. You just doing what you're doing and abiding by the new growth, when it comes to your self-control within self-preservation, is all the volume you need and speaks louder of you as a person.

The growth and overall amount of control you now have over things you didn't use to show would tell me everything I need to know if I were around you, and I'd probably stop whatever I was doing because I realized that you no longer allowed things to frustrate you quickly, and you were more approachable. Some people will continuously get worked up and rowdy. That's just a trait in some people that they have to want to come out of, and hopefully reading this will help you work on yourself; that's the primary key!

A perfect example that emphasizes what I mean when it comes to this type of behavior is more on a psychological mindset level, meaning it is all a mind game. I used to see the frustration in people; better yet, in things. I'd continuously pick at it and vice-versa, when someone did the same to me and say things that were subliminally directed then I would light up like a firecracker. When you grow from that, like I've grown tremendously, you'll now look at things that people do and realize it's attention-seeking, and it'll be pretty annoying but funny in the process. You'll recognize the things that used to get to you no longer do. You will notice for yourself that whoever is doing those same or similar activities has some personal insecurities of their own.

I believe that it'll only become more of a challenge because you're then stubborn and continuous in your ways. No matter how many times you've continued to run into that brick wall, you'll still lead in the same direction. So if one method does not work, let us try another sense of direction and so forth. And unfortunately, as I've stated before, you have some who may or may not be you where you are content, so you'll still find others trying to upset you and find yourself needing to conquer the challenges that still haunt you most.

It would be best if you wanted what you are willing to find in someone else for yourself. You must accept the positive just as quickly as you contain the negative. If you keep your eyes open, you will slowly realize that the negatives are so easy because it does not take much work to fulfill a gloomy hole.

Meanwhile, to relax in the positive of something takes time, effort, dedication, and overall devotion. It takes guidance and could mean perhaps grasping hold of yourself and letting go of someone else, whether it is one or more persons.

Sometimes you could come back around, and sometimes you something is too lost to be found, whether within you or within someone else. Sometimes you could find yourself letting go of something and end up meeting the ones you left after a long time, after all of you bettering yourselves, but having had to distance yourselves from one another first. And sometimes you finish the race leaving no one behind you and you are the only one out, but you cannot let yourself down, so you continue through the finish line. Here are so many shapes and forms of reality, as well as challenges in your preservation within the self and overall self-love.

You never want to negatively impact anything, which is why you always shoot for the stars and take the accountability and credibility that's installed into you. Be the difference, be that continuous change that you think is too good to be true. You feel that change is impossible because it is you.

Although you believe you can, you never thought you could. I want to be the person who says, "I told you so," after realizing you've read this passage. And every bit of it helped you work on yourself, and work on others in the process. It helped install that extra boost in your persona.

It helped you get through the days that used to drag and now wake up mastering dreams and thoughts and live your word! I want to see everyone grow and come out of the person they once were and feel like they must be. I want to see people come out of the person they feel like they have to be to survive, and realize if it's not helping you, if it's a continuous setback and you don't feel like you're moving up incredibly, take that challenge and boost yourself up to a brighter you. I never want people to feel like they're closed and boxed in and too young or old for change. I feel like self-preservation, which is the entitlement of this chapter, goes a long way.

Preserve your livelihood to master something on this earth that you haven't fully taken seriously. Knowing that you still have time for change every day and that sometimes it's honestly a matter of changing for the better - this could play a massive role in your life. You never want to have the thoughts behind you of not using your time wisely and trying to touch those you might have wanted to touch, or goals you've had the continue what-ifs of reaching without the dedication to do so.

I honestly believe that everyone has a plan and talent, and a task. To use the time you have wisely plays all the parts. Never take anything for granted, and overall never fault yourself for where you are now. Never look back at things that you're not willing to change, unless you're willing to not only make but be that change. Never think about the what-ifs and wonders of what something will or should be like, if you're only going to let those creative thoughts go to waste and into the hands of someone else.

Don't complain later, saying that you either thought the same or want credit for something you implied but never took the time to actually do. And that's what this book itself will tell you about, or at least bring you some peace within yourself about, so that the understanding of others and the outcomes, good or bad, will have more of a positive impact than a negative one at all costs.

When you direct self-preservation into your daily life, you're protecting yourself from any tendencies that harm could bring amongst you or within you because you're keeping yourself preserved. Out of harm's way, you are picking and choosing your battles wisely.

SELF-PRESERVATION

BEFORE reading this chapter.

1. What does the meaning of self-preservation mean to you?

_____

_____

_____

_____

_____

_____

2. If you didn't know and had to guess or even if you do know what the meaning of preservation is, what are 3 words that describe the word preservation?

_____

_____

_____

_____

_____

_____

3. Do you consider yourself to be a self-preserving person; if so, why or why not?

_____

_____

_____
_____
_____
_____

4. What is something that you need to forgive yourself for?

_____
_____
_____
_____
_____
_____

5. What are your core strengths within yourself?

_____
_____
_____
_____
_____
_____

AFTER reading this chapter

1. Does your understanding of self-preservation still mean the same after you've read the chapter vs. before reading the chapter?

_____
_____

_____
_____
_____
_____

2. Now that you understand the meaning behind the word self-preserve. Do you feel like you're self-preserving?

_____
_____
_____
_____
_____

3. What does your ideal day look like?

_____
_____
_____
_____
_____

4. On a scale from 1-10, how happy are you with your life right now?

_____
_____
_____
_____
_____

5. Are the obstacles in your life real, or did you make them up? In other words, do you feel as though you are your true self or living in uncertainty?

_____

_____

_____

_____

_____

_____

CHAPTER 3
SELF-SERVICE

"You have options; you have to decide on how you're going to go about them. You might like some things, and then you have some that you may not like or approve of, whether for that given day or at that given time. There's more to the outcome of things and consequences, whether good or bad, have a cause in effect. The sacrifices we choose play a huge role in our lives, and it is up to you to determine which are to stay and which are to put away. Not everything needs to come with you. Whether you believe it or not, every day you're considered to be a sacrifice. Due to choices made whether they have your approval or not, so self-sacrifice yourself for the beneficial reasons of self without questions asked as you would for that of someone else."

-INicole Royce

The self-service of self is the meaning behind dedicating what is needed of one to be the best that they can be to excel in the most positive way possible. One who uses "self-service" in their daily life projection will prosper into more than what the ordinary person will seek to overcome. Let us ask ourselves what self-service is.

Self-service is doing yourself the benefit of service within something; in this case, anything revolving around you and those around you. Those who could either positively or negatively impact you, and how to go about those situations wisely without making any judgments or decisions based on unsettled emotions.

I'd like to say that self-service plays a considerable role in commitment, giving yourself the ownership and overall self-respect that is needed. It would help if you gave yourself that own accountability and credibility. When someone commits to something, it puts that person in an embarrassing state of mind, allowing them to self-alleviate themselves. Of course, you handled the case in the way you felt was right. When, initially, you could've probably dealt with the situation differently, but you made decisions out of spite. You know the outcome of the problem will have a negative result.

Meanwhile, the outcomes result in backfires, and you are left feeling embarrassed and do not know how to admit or take that ownership for reacting out of spite. That is then when you allow yourself to self-alleviate. To alleviate yourself means letting go of that build-up stress, guilty conscience, that heavy burden that you're possibly carrying that's barely tolerable, leading you to want some sense of relief and for it, all to go away and just come to a halt. But yet you're not giving yourself that self-service, and to complete that phase you have to be able to consider that ownership that you know means well, not because you want to but because it's just the right way to go about things.

Be honest within yourself. It's best to put your sense of character beside yourself and lead by example for what you truly stand for. It is the result that matters most. It is how you handle and choose to go about a situation. Self-service is vital amongst you and those around you, whom you'll encounter on different levels. The more you find yourself within and manage this characteristic, the more you will relate to many others on so many different levels.

Most importantly, you'll discover the true you. When you self-service yourself, you'll know how to interact; And how not to interact. In most cases, you won't have to bother interacting at all. By eliminating all types of mixed emotions and possible distractions, you're trying to avoid things that aren't worth the energy or time that you put into them that could make you turn backward. The creation and what a certain someone can accomplish is beyond the extraordinary.

There are no boundaries for leveling up on a service requiring you to conquer yourself better. Once you've accomplished understanding the meaning of yourself and what you as a person genuinely stand for, everything will show and tell its way into your reality, leaving you to see nothing less than what's highly revolved after you begin to evolve. So why don't you give yourself a bit of self-service?

Have you ever honestly sat back and realized that you're using more energy elsewhere than you've once dedicated to yourself within, feeling as though you've accomplished nothing when indeed you've done above and beyond? Meanwhile, it is easy for you to think that you've yet to accomplish anything because you see nothing to show for it; but someone else can see your work. People can see your uplifting and withholding against what you want, have, and what you know you truly deserve. But you are still second-guessing yourself. As you will continue to do until you're able to see what's laid out on the table for you as someone else already sees within you, it's just the matter of you understanding yourself and seeing the gift you have as being your own.

It is up to you to inspire yourself to open your eyes and see that the only opinion that truly matters is one of a million vs. your own. What gift can multiple people see which you do not seek? It is highly honoring of someone to see the assistance you hold and are carrying, but it's more meaningful coming from yourself. I need you to see and believe in the gift you own and the power that you don't give yourself credit for within the days you live.

What will it truly take for you, as your person, to recognize the worth you have as you do to give someone else? The recognition that you seek within them? These are all things that everyone asks themselves better, yet these are rational statements that they partially believe but do not fully understand. Have you ever had a moment where you second-guessed yourself due to not having a complete understanding?

Meanwhile, you second guess yourself, but you honestly already have the answer deep down. At times, I am that same person with the wandering thoughts you have, and there is absolutely nothing wrong with that! You must never forget the steps, and admitting is critical. When you understand entirely, you will never have to question. Nor will you ever be in doubt; your understanding of worth will always fill you with certainty instead of uncertainty. It is the best feeling to have, but living and learning is the only way towards growth, so why not do better and lead by what you missed out on yesterday? You should take from that and continue through to the next day with something even better, which is a certainty after questioning.

After you realize and see the picture for being more than what it's projected, you will come to a sense of more places than just one. When you look at something not just for what it is but what it could be, should be, or would've been if only someone like yourself took the time to give it another objective, then everything will have more of the ability for growth. We're already capable, so why unable our truth in capability. Reaching for the stars is an understatement, yet we don't. We stare up in the sky and dream about it, sitting back, wishing for the highest level but feeling like it's too high to achieve.

Give Yourself A Pat on The Back

Why do we question ourselves? Why do we doubt our achievements towards certain success levels? We know our full potential, but then have a sense of stage fright when it comes to executing just that. So let's try something new along this self-service journey and overall becoming yourself. And give yourself the proper respect that you know you deserve for a change and do something different than you did just yesterday, just a couple of hours, minutes, and even seconds ago from now, and reach for the stars. I want you to go for the everlasting, knowing there are no limits.

Because you choose to imitate your growth ability, there would be no space for an opportunity if growth were nonexistent. If the option did not exist, there would be limitations towards success. Without knowing the true meaning of success, it substantially enables one to feel as though they have the same access pass towards success as others in the same circumstances as their person. Those who can relate are willing to listen to something other than what you believed to know. Hopefully, this will help those of you become even more significant than the person you already have molded to be just by allowing me to speak to you and truly help guide one to speaking life into existence.

The idea of self-service is to potentially help you. So you can be heard as much as you want a listening ear. I've been in the situation of feeling unheard. I've been in the position of not seeing what's right in front of me. Meanwhile, you have all answers right in front of you and just don't know what order to put them in. All simply because I was too stubborn to admit, too self-conscious to believe and open up, too in denial to question myself, or even have a sense of second-guessing anyone's opinion was better than the lack of my own. And with a mind-frame as such, you'll never get anywhere.

Because of that, you'll forever have a brick wall that seems to be getting in your way every time you thought you broke right through. An ongoing full force and yet running directly into another wall that you'll then try to figure out again. How can you break through? If you only sit back, observe, listen, and not be as quick to speak, you could probably learn how to avoid all the disturbances and go around it all.

I'm not saying that you won't have anything fighting your way slowing down your success, but getting through successfully, responsibly, and understanding instead of taking things more for granted will put a person in a much better headspace. Before it is too late is the key; it is never too late. To say that it is never too late is going against the definition that all we have in our world is time. That is all true, but time is valuable. The value of timeshares is the dedication that someone must do better to create something different from yesterday, show and give leadership and invest that reasonable amount of time in something worthwhile, rather than just for a while.

All of this leads to the definition of time wasted to meaning that your self-service isn't for seeking what your real value of life dramatically is. You as a person who's given life should be appreciated. Take a long look inside the meaning behind self-service.

- **Do you serve yourself?**
- **Do you foresee who you indeed are without the belief of anyone else telling you to make you feel whole?**

Following your thoughts, the meaning behind your-self and directly speak the 'I' or 'you'. Allow yourself to believe your energy that is being entered and released from within or throughout. It is always good to have con-firmation, but honestly, the only confirmation that matters is from you. It is easy for someone to tell you how they feel, whether they mean it or not, and of course, we all hope that someone is speaking positivity amongst us all, but we know that is not always the case. I say that com-prehensive self-service needs to be the protective coating that someone has in the pure belief of themself within themselves, no matter what someone else feels, thinks, or speaks upon, whether it's high or low.

It would help if you always were your most uplifting motivation first and foremost before anything. You should always self-service yourself, whether it's going out, cook-ing for yourself at home, or pampering yourself; even if it's just you doing absolutely nothing. Do this using the time of day in which you'd generally sit around or assure that other satisfactions were met besides your own. It's a must that you follow the qualities of what you truly stand for as a person without being lost within yourself.

Know that you're owed just as much as the next with-out any doubt, and truly understand and gain the meaning of what self-service stands for. Believe what you now know. It either feels right, or you think there's no way out, in which you've grown to become comfortable in a situa-tion for who knows how long.

The moment you're ready to self-service yourself,

you'll know when that time comes. You'll learn how to dodge the bullets and the walls that try and cave in on you. In between, you'll know how to not only knock down what's in your way, and learn going around and just re-routing on you a different path, either remembering or let-ting it all fade away as a lesson learned and a thought that you'd never forget. But never will you let it rule you as you've done once before; maybe even more times than others. Everyone has a story, and how you end is what matters most. You must be willing and open to change.

The change can be correct, yet very much could be misinterpreted just as suddenly as it was directed to you all because you were not ready. But it doesn't mean it's not going to come around again; it just means you weren't pre-pared at that moment to take on the challenge that you needed. This could've only been a couple of extra steps to help raise you towards your shine of greatness.

Once you allow yourself to finally open and prosper, you'll feel it within not only yourself but the heart of oth-ers with whom you'll come into contact. You will then know the difference between those who want to be like you and those who have similar qualities.

The quality of self-service could be anything, from getting away from people as a whole to being yourself; and finding out not only who you are, what qualities and characteristics you have, but what you stand for, and what purpose you carry along with you. These passages are in-credibly relevant for perusing a better you and overcom-ing things you felt were almost impossible to get through that turn out to be the most impactful thing yet. If nothing else is learned from this passage behind self-service and the overall meaning, it plays a role in every aspect of life that we somehow intertwine.

The purpose behind this word of self-service goes far; it goes beyond words that everyone speaks. I love to stress the meanings behind anything revolving around the word self. And the utmost importance behind the name and what it carries.

Sometimes it is as if self no longer matters once you have reached a certain level or realized that the stories are pretty challenging to meet. Unfortunately, we are continuing our bullying when it comes to believing and letting ourselves down in the midst when we definitely should be our first and foremost priorities, no questions asked.

You can't bring something into the world and expect change if you haven't yet abided by the change within; you'll continuously have an issue if you don't fully come into the understanding of what and who you indeed are. So it's most important to fix yourself and decide what you want to do in a specific type of situation you're in, no matter what or which way you go, which route you decide to take, how long, or how short the ride.

There are an opening and an exit for every single life. And we are to use that remorse and take overall accountability in our self-service of change; that circle of life that we hope to go around. We as people must not ponder over it or lead the way to the drought but seek the way and uplift, leading to empowerment and opportunity. The sources are out there. The wave is ready for you to ride. It's all a matter of whether or not you're prepared to change. Are you indeed ready to be that difference that you always talk about most? Follow the thoughts that are on your mind? You are probably filled with constant what -ifs and how comes; try turning all of that into wishful thinking. And see where that process leads you and see how powerful you become. This information I am sharing with you is all from experience.

There is nothing that I would lead one to believe that I did not project and conquer within myself first. To share and spread knowledge towards something that I feel those around me could use to help their growth placement. I am all for it and willing to share. To hope that this information helps indeed without a doubt. But if it doesn't, or there's something else that I can help you with. I sure hope that this passage helps you through. I hope that any questions or thoughts hindering you will soon no longer. Because everything that I feel will connect with your balance, your inner person is right here in your hands.

The ball is practically in your court; now, it is time for you to work. That willpower that it takes to want in or want out and how bad you want it. Everyone has their thoughts on their ways of doing things, and their outcomes could either end up the same for better or worse. You can get a second go-around, or it could be the only chance that you get. But we all want indefinite change and welcome new beginnings and overall accomplishments. Suppose you believe in yourself just as much as the next person.

Then you're in continuously good hands and will take something with you every day.

Dedication and Deliverance

There will always be a part in this reading that will regularly answer the questions you seek. I never failed to ask myself and never hesitated to ensure that I abided by getting the answers in some way, shape, or form. Until I gained a sense of understanding I always keep pushing and striving forward. There will always be questions, and there will always be answers. It is just a matter of finding the most accurate solution subsidizing your question. Forever remain humble. Keep your head held high. And remember that every move we make, every risk that we take, we're only in competition with ourselves.

Nothing rushed will be accounted for if not appropriately handled. You can lose something just as quickly as you've gained it, so always remember to take yourself with care and the knowledge you have that leads you to be where you are. I'd say you should start by brainstorming and doing a process of elimination before maybe either doing or saying something, whether directed to someone or something that relates to you and your concerns, or just your typical daily well-being.

I say brainstorming allows you to get a sense of your thoughts and immediately tune into your inner self. I know it will enable me to weigh out the pros and cons against situations and things and ideas that I have. It allows me to either explore, keep it within myself, or will-

71

ingly share the vision or multiple thoughts that I could be thinking without thinking. The moment you begin to find your true within yourself, you'll see that many things that happened won't be so quick to happen. Many things that have happened could've had a much brighter outcome or a well-thought-out process.

I'm slowly learning to grasp what it means to do things for yourself and keep your sanity, no matter how much you do for others. If you aren't properly kept up and taken care of, then nothing will ever seem to matter. It only half matters without the full effect, because you will continue to have that constant reminder of what you could've done. It all seems to boil over when you hit a rough patch.

When something you have done could have had a different outcome, you noticed nobody around to pick up where you left off when you picked them up.

The urgency of things is additional. Everyone is different; that is why we must continue to build within ourselves and mold ourselves differently than just to what our world expects us to be. If you realize our world expects all these things, only certain things are limited to learning.

While most things taught throughout life throughout school are the fundamental mind stages, the real learning stages do not exist unless someone leads it to you, brings it to your attention, or are simply from experience.

Anticipating Your Pieces Beyond Exception

Some things, although they're taught to you, may still leave you with the missing pieces at times. Sometimes more than most, you have to get to the bottom of the mystery yourself and fill in the blanks left behind. It takes a specific mind frame and stage of mind to find what to search for precisely. It has everything to do with your guidance and everything to do with your potential for wanting something. It would help if you never let your upbringing or lack of knowledge determine or have any judgment on your self-service outcome. The sky is the limit, so reach for the universe as I like to say and never take no for an answer. I've always abided by this, and even until this day I do not believe in the word "No." I believe in maybe later, and I'll try and figure it out. We can see what we can do, or possibly I'll see what I can do. But never will anyone hear me flat out say no due to embitterment within myself.

The only time that I will say no is when you can genuinely see that someone is not reaching their highest, and you know they are capable of so much more. And then you have many who hear the word no and get discouraged while I, of course, was that person, and soon became uplifted or motivated. I like to stress that everyone is different but could have the same result. Never allow your situations to dictate your success's outcome.

If anything that ever interferes and gets in the way of your peace pathways, your guidance tracks, and you do not want to be disturbed, it's OK to tune it out or take an alternate route. It's also OK to not deal with any of it at all and to avoid it altogether - everything you feel is a distraction to you and your power until you're either able to handle it wisely, or even if it genuinely means just not having anything to do with it is outstanding.

Whichever way one chooses to go about something, how they handle the situations is your choice. The only guidance that I am giving is the guidance to self. When things start to affect you, they then affect your bright outcome and that future you have that you'll either put on hold or never look to reach all; because you've given up or felt as if you weren't worthy. And it is for everyone to know their worthiness.

To self-service yourself brings much deeper love than just doing things for you.

The smallest things get into the mental stages and the controlled mind frames we hold because we are all different. Some of them are stubborn, some have a balance, and some more are easily influenced. It is not by choice. The only way they know is how they have been guided, led, and directed to believe that is the right way. Those of you who had hardships in guidance, of course you probably thought it was wrong, or the situations weren't right. Still, until you know that it's either right or wrong, you want to, of course, believe that the people who you've followed and who looked over you throughout those years are in your best interests. When you realize that is not the case, it then becomes problematic.

It becomes worse than the situations of others which could drastically change. You are not alone, nor do you have to experience individual experiences alone. Many people go through these hardships of not knowing themselves yet are the brightest of them all. I believe that the worse your income, the better your outcome.

I understand that the more experience you have within life, no matter how rough, hard, or rugged it might have been, those outcomes and how you made it have all the lessons within that you've learned. You know what is wrong, you know what is right, but just not how to put it together or even the sense of how to express that feeling. Sometimes things are said, whether aggressive or in silence, or even despite someone being the quietest. But believe me you, I hear every single one of your cries. No matter how much pride you have within, which is positively amazing, everyone can be knocked down to express the feelings they remain held and locked away inside. And to those of you who are reading who can relate, I genuinely hope to grasp hold of you someday.

There is no day like the day you live. Remember that there is an in the same way there is an out. Each story's situations and outcomes have their beginnings, but no matter how hard, the endings are entitled to remain just as strong. To everyone, please remember to give yourself the service you need. Take each step one at a time and do not rush a virtue. You must remember that patience outweighs it all, and by reading, you're taking those steps needed to assure that you're in the right direction required and be of the consistent reminder that you're doing a DAMN GOOD JOB at it because you're taking those steps. You are already prospering, and you do not even know it yet! Continue to fill and uplift your thoughts by hearing motivational words, quotes, and phrases in the positive so that your mind can get accustomed to favorable positions instead of negative informalities.

When your mind regularly hears negative things, your body believes they're true, and you begin to live negatively. When you feed yourself positivity, your circle will become pure. And those around you will start to disappear. Remember that misery sure loves its company, and that is a fact. But if positivity is your surrounding, your discomfort will then seize up.

JOURNAL

SELF-SERVICE

BEFORE reading the chapter

1. What does self-service mean to you when it comes to one of your qualities of life?

_____
_____
_____
_____
_____
_____

2. Do you use self-service where you'd like to be or where you'd like to be and interested in extending your next milestone.

_____
_____
_____
_____
_____
_____

3. What are some changes that you've discovered or made in your life up until now?

_____
_____
_____
_____

4. What are your five-year goals from now as a self-service to yourself? Whether you're not where you'd like to be, moderately 1.) What does self-service mean to you?

_____
_____
_____
_____
_____
_____

5. Do you consider yourself doing what you truly want to do?

_____
_____
_____
_____
_____
_____

AFTER reading the chapter.

1. Does the meaning of self-service mean the same to you after you've read the chapter than before?

_____
_____
_____
_____
_____
_____

2. Do you have any discomfort or regrets about yourself? Maybe something you took for granted about self-servicing within yourself that you wish you could undo and renew?

_____

_____

_____

_____

_____

_____

3. What big changes do you want to make in your life?

_____

_____

_____

_____

_____

_____

4. Which dream would you want to consider and invest in if you had the open opportunity to choose whatever you'd like for your dreams to pursue?

_____

_____

_____

_____

_____

_____

5. What are the biggest setbacks of you not being able to fulfill your goals and life long dreams?

_____

_____

_____

_____

_____

_____

CHAPTER 4
SELF-GUIDANCE

"Make sure to be your own. It's easy to be influenced by those around you rather than a person of themself. Everyone wants a role model or person to mirror. Why don't you apply the feelings you would like to feel and be that original within yourself for a change? Not every example is good, and not every bad example is negative. Sometimes we have lessons for viewpoints from all angles. And it's up to you to self-guide. Give yourself the guidance you're gifted to have and eliminate the distractions. Be your certainty for once, no second-guessing. To live for you; abide by the cause to your effects. And choose your answer being your guide to the ending of your story to tell."

-INicole Royce

The urgency of self-guidance. The intake and the outcome of self-guidance. Let us try asking ourselves what self-guidance is. I am truly sure that I understand what self-guidance is. Let us start by asking ourselves the basics behind self-guidance questions and the exact problem of, "What is self-guidance?" when referring to a person of self. When I teach myself the basics of self-guiding, I must tune into my inner peace and voice.

I must find things that help me focus and catch concentration within my mind and the situations I place myself into, or remove myself from. When you are trying to find your inner peace, that's something that you must find within based on your likes and dislikes, calm, triggers, uplifts, and weaknesses. You must find the center of you and what makes or breaks you, and pretty much be in complete tune with your body and mind. It took quite some time with me trying to do the same when it comes to me and situations that I deal with daily, so those are just a few ways that I discovered works for me.

Meanwhile, they do not always work for everybody, but choose which best leads you. I believe that certain things come with clues, and with hints come a sense of reality. Even though each clue you receive will not always have the exact meaning and understanding you are look-ing for, it is up to you to read in between the lines. I look at this as something that gets deeper over time and throughout your experiences, because it's honestly the ex-perience and situations you have been through and over-come that allow you to become in tune with yourself. It could be helpful, threatening, or indifferent; not always cheerful but not hostile. It could just be something that triggers you to find that self-guidance within.

To Every Good Isn't Bad; And For Every Bad Isn't Ugly.

From my experiences, I never like to say that any of mine were terrible situations. They were mainly situations that I wanted to dislike that I eventually learned to love as I grew older. Now I have more sense of understanding about something and why it either happened or didn't happen. Depending on what you put yourself through, things will naturally come with specific situations. Maybe if you haven't found your inner voice with things and become in tune, you will tolerate the self-guidance level that your life has put you through less, causing you to have a short fuse because you're feeling trapped about how to go about it.

As we get older, we think we're running out of time when self-guidance has no time. Whenever you reach that level of maturity, you'll realize that you've always had that tactic the entire time. Things will try their best to blindside you more because of the level of tolerance you've set for yourself. I believe that everything has its time. And in due time, things will find their way, and so will you. I never like people to feel like they must rush time, but there is always a limit, although time is limitless. All those questions you should ask yourself throughout these chapters will help you get through what you are going through. This isn't a lecture, but walks you through every obstacle you are going through or coming across.

I want to touch each person that I possibly can along the way who's questioning their daily devours but can't; because they're in constant reminder of how behind they genuinely are or think they are. So, in all honesty, if you're reading this book or even having these continuous thoughts, I want to say that you're on the right path because you take the time to figure out how to move forward. I highly consider all of this a start to your beginning to get where you're going. And it can all be made possible.

Take notes from someone who's in the same position and who's put a helping hand out, hoping to touch the minds and get into the minds of those in the question of self. After all, I never let go of things or people blocking my growth because I felt like that level wasn't the level for me when in reality, it's never just the matter of what you know that plays a huge effect, but who you know.

The resources you have do not limit you from having the same opportunities you could give to someone else; it's all a matter of being at the right place at the right time, and persistence rules everything. I like to say when in doubt, go for it, because it's your most risk-taking moments that prove to you that situations and circumstances aren't always as bad as the outcome that people may place over your head to be. Everyone is different, and every outcome is different. What works for one with 100% will NOT work for someone else, and if it does, it could either take a toll for the better or worse in many situations.

My overall mission behind the statement that I just made is that everyone is on their own timing. To be compliant within yourself and have that self-guidance given that will determine the positive outcome, you must maintain the control you have within your mind to resolve the matter. For others to seek the same potential that you wish to see within yourself, you have to not only want it, but drive yourself into better conditions and situations without a handout.

You never mislead your trend of thinking for something temporary you place your mind in the directions you wish to go in, and you strive towards the top and remain consistent within. The meaning of self-guidance is powerful. With responsibility comes maturity, and maturity overall comes from experience. Having experience within something will set you to knowing how something should be abided by and what it takes to get there.

You can successfully stabilize yourself and understand the true definition of self-guidance, and how your self-guidance can lead you to your determination. So can choices made continuously of you with the judgment and constructive criticism of others only pushing you forward, instead of holding you back, keeping you in what feels to be situations of restraint. The only opinions that truly matter are yours.

I stand behind these words when I say that your intake determines the outcome given. Many may or may not agree, but I'm a walking example. Although I won't touch everybody, I'm pretty positive that I'll graciously have the pleasure of connecting with those of you who are willing to take that next step. Those of you who are eager to take that extra mile and are not content with being content. Those who are not just comfortable with being comfortable and willing to want more out of life than what's given to you or that you feel like you can reach. Everyone is entitled to the same race. It is just a matter of how you decide to finish. And even then, would you consider yourself done?

Take Advantage of Your Control

Once you start, you can only keep going because of the natural adrenaline in you to excel. The drive of accomplishing just that will lead you to want more out of what you're putting into something. I like to say that each topic not only helps you but allows you to also look into the help of others, reaching out to those who are either calling out or not saying anything at all.

When you have genuinely found yourself and your gift, it becomes a natural resource, and you will help those without intentionally doing so. Everything will soon come naturally. That is what self-guidance consists of - knowing when, how, and where to either lend a helping hand or sit back and observe before you go headfirst into something. It will help you determine what is needed and what is not, whether dealing with yourself or someone else. You have to realize that most of the things we get upset about as human beings are things we have complete control over.

You can't help but worry about things you have no control over because it's instinct at times. But you have control over your mind, which determines the direction and how you choose to go about it. You can either make a situation better, or worsen a problem because you have let go of your self-guidance.

Most situations are not going to be fair but train yourself, and train your mind into the thought process of overcoming it.

If we set our thought process up for success, situations won't be as hard to handle or overcome. Because once you're entirely in trust with yourself and know your mind, you won't be as sensitive to situations you know exist and circumstances that you have no control over.

I like to say that self-guidance is a considerable emotion because it has a significant impact on how people react, respond, and are resourceful. I like to say that self-guidance has gone a long way for me when figuring things out and the differences between going through and getting through. I used to feel as if I was continuously wasting my time, no matter how much help I got.

Nowadays, people are so content with a helping hand. They're almost unable to self-guide themselves into a positive response instead of a negative. An answer determines an outcome that someone either can't get out of or has to put themselves in due to a simple mistake. Most things that happen can go two ways. One way good, the other not so good; but how you approach or react could determine a lot of that.

An example for example

I'm going to give you an example that I've experienced to help break down what I'm saying: I'm currently 27 years old. And my entire life, I've felt like I'm belittling myself and cutting myself short from what I not only know I deserve but what I feel like I'm capable of because I'm either seeing something someone else is doing, have done, or where they're going.

I've had the helping hands of my family and family friends closest to me.

However, they helped place the words of wisdom, and continuous guidance set the words of wisdom and constant advice. Throughout the years and over time from my mother, the woman closest to me, I would not trade her advice for anything in the entire world. It seems like I have never listened, but in all reality, with everything within me, I see myself mirroring this woman every single day. It leaves the question of my mother saying to me, "Wow, you have been listening, or you remind me of myself when you do this." Once you find your genuine defined person behind self-guidance, you'll respond to the many situations you're in touch with along the way.

Your outcome will determine just that it's all about your approach; it's about your mind, body, and how you go about things you come across and sometimes not every time. Still, more time than most, you'll realize that how you choose to handle something could've worsened it. You had to become one with the outcome because you made the self-guidance decision and controlled the situation.

The role of self-guidance is huge! It helps you out a lot; you will not react as much or react as needed. You will learn to either sit back and watch or turn the other cheek, leaving whatever it is that could hinder you in the dark to become another situation elsewhere. Most of all, self-guidance helps you with any and everything that you come across each day.

Of course, you'll have those moments where you come away and feel like you've messed up by saying something you probably shouldn't have or doing something you probably shouldn't have.

All in all, having self-guidance will allow you to overcome that situation and come back from and accept whatever challenges come your way. The levels of the challenges are what are going to get you, and you're going to have plenty, so never think it's over; it'll just be much easier to take them on as they come.

As a constant reminder to yourself, it's always you that holds the ball in your court, and you should never take the blame for someone else's wrongdoing and place it over yourself. All of us have a choice, and it is a matter of how we go about that decision. Whether it means not responding right away or even responding at all. To each his own, everyone's self-guidance will have a different direction. We are all looking to reach the top. And no matter which way you go at the end of the road, if you get there is what truly matters most. Do not always look at downfalls as bad; look at them as either a lesson learned or lessons still to be learned. Sometimes you must leave things behind to lead, and sometimes you must get left behind to catch up. Not everything has bad intentions because of its timing, but everyone's timing has a deadline, and it is how you meet it at the end that truly counts.

There is no one to judge w how you do something if it is your best way of doing it. While moving forward through this stage, do not turn back; continue with your head high and use the walls you have run into along the way as a minor setback for better, never for worse. I like to tell everyone to consider those mistakes a helping hand instead of a downfall, because what is a lesson learned with no errors?

What are helping hands when you have always only had a handout? I like to encourage people, even myself, throughout time because I steadily practice what I preach. You should most definitely start encouraging yourself more and being mindful of the epic fails you feel are a turn for the worse, and utilize that same energy of emotion as more encouragement!

If you do not understand the ideas of self-guidance, it is OK to slow yourself down, ask questions, or rewind to gain a sense of mind. Many of us think that we know, but we genuinely don't. And it's OK to say that we don't know or need help with something instead of feeling as if we've got it. Some things are OK, but it's OK not to take on the load completely alone. Still, there's a fine line between knowing what's of importance and what's not, and picking and choosing things wisely when it comes to your motives. In this case, self-guidance should be controlled and taken advantage of. Some situations may tick us off; problems that cause us to either be able to or not be able to bite the bullet and hold our tongue.

These are situations in which we either have control, gain control, or completely lose it all. But the self-guidance kicks in when we can read that sense of urgency. That level of guidance either tells us yay or nay instead of going back to what ifs and how comes, and you shouldn't keep going back to what you possibly should've done.

JOURNAL

SELF-GUIDANCE

BEFORE reading the chapter

1. What is self-guidance?

_____
_____
_____
_____
_____
_____

2. Are you completely understanding the meaning of what self-guidance truly holds?

_____
_____
_____
_____
_____

3. What are some of the characteristics that self-guidance holds?

_____
_____
_____
_____
_____
_____

4. Do you consider yourself to be one who serves a quality as someone who has self-guidance?

_____

_____

_____

_____

_____

_____

5. Talk about a time that you last did something for the first time that was for yourself?

_____

_____

_____

_____

_____

_____

AFTER reading the chapter

1. Does self-guidance still hold the same meaning to you after reading the chapter as it did before reading the chapter?

_____

_____

_____

_____

_____

_____

2. Do you feel confident in the true meaning behind self-guidance?

_____

_____

_____

_____

_____

_____

3. What are now some of your self-guided characteristic goals?

_____

_____

_____

_____

_____

_____

4. After reading this chapter. Do you feel as though you serve a quality as someone who could now possibly become self-guided?

_____

_____

_____

_____

_____

_____

5. What is something that you'll do for yourself from now on that will positively benefit your life circumstances?

_____

_____

_____

CHAPTER 5
SELF-DISTURBANCE

"If there's something you truly want, you'll do whatever it takes to get it. To realize that doing whatever it takes means keeping it. Don't do things on impulse but because you are interested in becoming sensible towards things that have your attention. The disturbances try to distract you and knock you off your game, your focus, your tunneled vision. It's a distraction not needed - discipline yourself to tune things out. Selective hearing is directed more towards interest instead of just potential interest. It's okay to pull back and turn the other cheek and find a streak as you lead to follow."

-INicole Royce

The gist of this chapter is about self-disturbance. The meanings behind self-disturbed individuals have already labeled themselves as multiple things around them that only they can understand. But you can always be the listening ear. You can be the listening ear of someone who has become self-disturbed, whether that someone is you or indifferent. There is always going to be something that disturbs you. And it is up to you to know how to treat and handle that situation. There are different signs to look out for, along with people to watch out for.

However, just like anything else, you have some

things that are okay to be addressed. And then you have something that no longer needs a response. In this matter, the disturbance of self is our head focus. Have you ever come in term with the phrase head focus? And better yet, know what it means? The word head focus has multiple understandings, but I perceive it to mean overall being in tune with your mind. To have thought consistency within yourself and attached to your instinct about things. Being head-focused allows people to see something that they probably have yet to see ever!

And secondly, something that will allow you to grow and realize more things that you never even knew existed, all because of that one minor setback leading to self-disturbance. To be a person of head focus is how I refer to myself in many situations. When I am head-focused, that is just me saying, "I am not as in my head as thought," and I can't get out of it. But I have tunnel vision, allowing nothing and no one to get in the way of my thought process of things or slow me down throughout the process of it all. For someone to become head-focused, they see everything going on around them, and they will even engage from time to time. Still, they never lose focus of their interest or intentions of where they see themselves being or, better yet, going at that given time.

Whether it's in the now or the path in the direction they lead to follow, when a person is head-focused, they're determined to do something. The determination to finish with the healthy mindset they had to start with to finish; and accept nothing less than that accomplishment. We've all had that time. Yet, some have more than others. Try asking yourself questions like: "How do I clear my head and focus?"

Better yet, "What does it mean to even be inside of my head at all?" These are both questions that people suffer daily, including myself. It comes to finding ways to clear your head and help yourself regain your mental peace. It takes little to nothing, no matter how difficult or challenging the situations you're going through are.

It is more like setting an obligation for yourself of a way out of what seemed almost to be no way. But you have to come up with creative ideas, and experience things that are either new to you or simply things that you probably enjoy doing that you hardly ever find the time to do. I'd say that you need to make time to struggle with these issues.

I must admit I have had quite the fair share of sustaining my mental peace and overall headspace to become more head-focused for my good. So, I cannot speak too much about what others experience or go through in their heads. Still, I know from my challenge of being in my head that maybe some of you can relate. And perhaps some could apply it to your situations.

Get out of your own way!

To be inside of my own head leads me to be looking back instead of not being able to look forward. I look ahead a little too much to where I've almost overwhelmed myself with the sense of action and overthinking trying to overcome any given situation—and making all things in a sense somewhat possible. It is like reaching for the stars and having that mental state overcome so many things, but not putting yourself in the successful ways.

Set yourself up for success. We can all have a dream, but how will you overcome that dream? What are you doing differently from the next person, to not maintain and overcome those dreams you seek? All that I'm saying is you must have a play in place. It is more than just thinking and talking about it, but what actions are being applied. And what steps have you taken to assure that you get to the level of where you're trying to be before you complain about which direction you are going in.

We all over-analyze things at times and a few more than others, and it could be okay at times. But in most cases, it is not okay at all, because you are probably pressuring yourself way too much! I know I have done so, and the feeling is not a pleasant one to have. These examples lead to self-consciousness, whether it is the feeling you have about something or the actions you project. It is always good to vent and be the listening ear at times instead of just needing continuous guidance. To guide is to lead by example too.

Of course, do unto others as you would want them to do unto you. Because without a doubt I, too, hold things in from time to time. Meanwhile, I look for a way out in my book by giving, sharing, and overall caring, which could sometimes end up being way too much sometimes because that is what comes with a big heart. There must be a balance whether anyone likes it or not. But what's essential is to try asking yourself these questions: "What do I like? "Does this make me happy? "What is self-disturbance?"

The meaning behind self-disturbance is when you cannot remain focused on what is needed of you to maintain a consistent task or even lifestyle. It is different for most and more effortless for some to become self-disturbed. While self-disturbed, you cannot guide yourself as quickly as you would have been if only if you would focus more on yourself. A lot is going on in one's life, but some have more than others. Many things happen in people's lives, and you must learn to balance them. If there is no balance, there is no structure, and for every dedicated person, there's structure. The peace of mind in which you seek to lead for yourself and by the example for others.

Getting off track with things is quite common to have something come up beyond your self-control. However, you cannot ponder over things you have no control over.

There are indeed things that you have every bit of control over. I look at that as being mind over matter. I'm saying that when something happens or is happening or has ever happened in your life, most of the time we naturally stop what we're doing and help. This is an instinct, and slows us down entirely on our initial focus.

We might go back to our initial focus later. But more than likely, the average person brushes it under the rug and becomes sidetracked. I am not saying it is not good to help others by helping yourself, but you must balance.

Having or gaining the balance of something realistically is a natural human priority that most of us lack, and don't even notice because everything becomes routine. Have you ever tried to find a balance within your lifestyle and thought you'd found it?

You'll realize that you are going through the motions regularly so much that you forget what made you happy or most enjoyed. This starts to make you angry because you finally get the gist. And you see how you are probably not the self you once knew, and are annoyed with yourself of because of your own mental space. And in some cases, this could mean you are in a better cognitive area, so you are grateful to have grown. As well as for some, it is like you are growing and have grown. But still seem to find yourself going around in circles with life and just not moving through it fast enough or as quickly as you probably intended. In these cases, you began to make yourself miserable and overthink it all with the conclusion of either making it better or worse or going straight towards the direction for the worse.

As I have stated before, my job for being so honest with you throughout this book is to allow you to envision yourself. There's always something that's going on. Someone who's trying to remain humble and hang tight starts to slip.

And that is something that truly breaks my heart and I would love to save many from that, whether it is in person or just touching you from lending me your listening ear. Think about this as if all of this we're going through it together. As you must know, I am molding myself while trying to help develop others. But, unfortunately, this world that we live in will not teach us the exact ways to pay attention to the clues that stand right in our faces every day.

There is absolutely no way to have better self-discipline than to find your focus. But, unfortunately, we get so caught up in a life of wanting to live the lifestyle. But we don't put in the actual work for it. We feel like what goes around should quickly come back around, without doing anything to accommodate the hardship of what it takes to earn it. So instead, we insist on trying to "Keep Up with the Joneses" when you do not know what led them to get there.

It would help if you tried asking yourself about the many times you focused on assuring that something is in the right light for someone else. Have you given yourself that same dedication? Have you focused on your peace the way you have led someone else to theirs? Or better yet, are you teaching them to calm themselves when you are nowhere near your own calm? It is not selfish by any means; it is pretty responsible for choosing yourself first. There has to be a point where you place just as much focus on your own happiness as you do outside because you're your only actual change, and no one else can make of you what you're capable of driving yourself. And why would you want another to gain the credibility of what you are capable of, if only you realized that you could most definitely accomplish and achieve?

I am sure to speak by experience and explain situations that have affected me, for things I've either gone through or still going through. And each of those things I've grown from while continuously growing within them. So, who is to say that you are not feeling the same and just not aware of your way out? You probably have questioned yourself about where you should even start to begin change. Whether it's what your daily routine consists of following self-discipline, self-care, self-consistency, self-structure, self-motivation; those things lead up to the meaning behind self-disturbance and without focusing on yourself.

As selfish as that sounds, it is the truth. You must know and understand the meaning behind finding your own happiness to create the way for another. At times we make way for another. Meanwhile, we go back into our withdrawal, and we become resistant and say the words: "I'm not doing this anymore for this certain someone," "I shouldn't have done this, "I could've done this and that this way. "

Although that is all true to say and better yet to feel you have every right, is it truly the feeling you are supposed to have while helping someone? It is easy to say those things out of spite when one is not self-disciplined. So a person needs to try asking themselves, "Am I mentally prepared to take on these challenges that could be bigger than my own?" Sometimes, the answer needs to be, "No." There are many ways to go about all of this - I'm finding my self-discipline and understanding the meaning behind my self-disturbance and why I'm in the same continuous spot as before. Not just in the physical form but mentally.

Don't Just Speak; Act on It!

I use myself as the prime example for my words. I feel that the things that I'm talking about and topics that I'm hitting against are things that are not going through only my head; there are plenty of others thinking about them. AI consider myself a leader - not in only what I say but by things that I do. Everything done on the outside looking in will never be what people perceive it to be.

There is always a story behind it, and that is what people need to understand. There is a way to get there if you want to get there. But you must take the proper steps to secure your course.

Securing your way is a wall you create that helps stabilize your thoughts of feeling safe and genuinely meaning it, and feeling free from all your worries and anxiety.

"What are the pros and cons of self-disturbance?" I ask myself these questions as I insist on gaining a more precise understanding and open thought process from all angles. To start with the bad and end with the good. Then, reality will speak the cons of self-disturbance. All by example, without you even having to do too much of anything to dodge the bullet.

Pros and Cons:

I want to say the cons of self-disturbance: we do not

like to let things go. We ponder over them by pondering over a situation or multiple situations that have yet to be truly resolved by doing so. We allow resilience to be grown whether it is for a day, a week, a couple of months, and even for years. We'll always beat ourselves up by pondering over what we could do, what we should've done, or what needs to be different. But we never stay on the path to abide by doing and completing what we know we need to do. It is easy to say you would like to accomplish this and that, but it's another thing actually to do it.

Have you ever just sat back and thought about a time or maybe even multiple times that you've been a helping hand for someone? Whether it be a close peer, a family member, a friend, or even your significant other, who probably wasn't as significant as you thought they'd turn out to be. To you it's what seems like the perfect gesture. But how many times did you apply the same energy for them as you've applied to yourself?

There are multiple times that I could use myself as a prime example of being in that trap. The feeling that I've been deceived and unfair against myself, causing me not only to realize that I was becoming taken advantage of, but also setting an unfair challenge against myself. By putting my own life on the back burner and not valuing my purpose and going against my goal. And whether you know or believe it, every one of us on this earth has a goal. It is just up to us to find it before it is too late. Many love to say that it is never too late, that all we have is time.

However, that logic is exceptionally accurate on so many levels. It contradicts itself as well. We indeed have the time, of course. Still, time does run out and sometimes sooner than for others. Sometimes quicker than you'd come to realize after realizing that you should've, could've, would've done things differently, and by that time, it's too late. I am a person who strongly believes in energy.

I have made the same mistake for decades at a time in my life. But what I can do is learn from them continuously, as I'm still doing each day, and also help lead others to seek their disturbances and self-worth. Every time you put something before yourself, you're offering yourself as a sacrifice instead of continuing to work on yourself.

Not many people can carry the weight of what I would like to say, "applying the same energy," to yourself as you would normally do for someone else. And sometimes, we as human beings give ourselves an unfair disadvantage and the short end of the stick during many different situations. And we are still too proud to admit to it, so we take it out on someone or something. Which then leads to hurting ourselves or hurting someone later. And we become at fault to compete against one another and even harder on ourselves. Because we know our capability and the many capabilities that we have, but we look back on all the years spent after realizing we have got nowhere in the process.

There's a difference between getting somewhere in the process and going through the process. There are plenty of times where I am going through the process, but getting somewhere in the process of life . By saying that, I am saying that I am still learning and placing myself in the spotlight that we all have the same thoughts and are uncertain of our actual way out. Many feel like their way of thinking is the only way. So we keep our thoughts to ourselves until we're overwhelmed. And they start to come out in a way that we wish we could take back, but by then, it's too late. Giving the withholding of becoming self-disturbed is like allowing someone to live the life you plant the seeds to live.

By saying that, I mean that you're allowing someone to either pick up the pieces or live the life of which you are to live within yourself. There are not many people who own up to the disturbances they seek. Many people fight it or make excuses, but there are those who speak on it and put their thoughts and judgment into action. The principles behind self-disturbances fall along the lines of uncertainty. As long as someone's uncertain, they will always have the urgency of those things, whether it's personal or objects or even events that occur, and which find the need to get in the way of what one has going at any given time place. As we get older and the days get wiser, you will learn how to handle your self-discrepancies once you take the steps towards learning your actual true self.

To become someone who begins to understand their true self is bigger than anything. The downfalls of disturbances could bring out a worse outcome than expected. It is more of the time, the place, and the overall setting that determines what it is that will self-disturb someone. I use myself, for example. There have been multiple times when someone says something that someone else feels the need to add their comment to. But it disturbs so I am either distant or become bothered by whatever it is they either choose to say or not to say. And in some cases, you have to deal with and open up another sense of thinking. That leads you to show that not everyone has the same thought process or urgency as you do.

There are multiple causes and effects to someone becoming self-disturbed. It takes a strong mind frame to understand that it's not just something you can overpower. Many of us out there are not aware of our disturbances or the disturbances caused by others.

Meanwhile, we as people have become too prideful to admit to these things. The cause of disturbances can be as little as your daily routine, and things that you feel are an obligation to you that you not only stand by but abide by. You may sometimes find yourself having to take ownership and accountability for when something truly has nothing to do with you. The gist of self-disturbance is making sure that you know how to discipline yourself. To find that own self-balance of not allowing anything to get in the way of your success, your vision.

It is okay to be selfish at times, but what is being selfish to better yourself if it means improving those around you in the long run? The characteristics of self-disturbance did not click in my mind growing up. I never understood how vital self-disturbance was as I didn't know how to control it properly. I used to look at self-disturbance as an excuse for why someone could do better, yet fail to realize that I had complete control over others when balancing things that could get me off track and off focus. I like to say that a few things that cause one to become stressed are your mental processes. You can break down into that positive mental headspace within and look into the eyes of self. To forgive but never forget people or things that may have disturbed you along the way.

I believe that from those people or things that were possibly in disturbance of you for every situation, there was a lesson learned, and without those effects, what good would it have been truthfully? Of course, you could make up thoughts and opinions, but what good are those thoughts and ideas with no sense of experience to put with them? Instead of blaming someone or finding someone to blame, you should see how it feels when you finally blame yourself and end up being your own self-guidance at the end of it all.

After realizing that I played a massive role in most things that I allow to hold an excuse for when it comes to things that get me off track, I understand myself now. It's more motivation to get onto myself because I'm my example of a perfectly imperfect model. When you start taking on your challenges for things other than to be good, bad, or indifferent and looking at the situations as uplifting or motivating yourself, you'll begin to have a different urgency in the way you do things. Whether in general or to people, you come across differently in the way you speak.

A Sense of Character

To become one with self-disturbance, you have to find a place in your mind that allows you to separate your thoughts personally. To know when and how to adjust within yourself. It's one thing to know little to nothing but absolutely without a doubt a significant problem to be of complete self-disturbance when it comes to knowing yourself. To lose yourself and be self-disturbed can cause you to become resentful towards things that you would never think would trigger you, whether it is your actions verbally, physically, or in thought. No matter the situation or the circumstance, there is a beginning to every ending and vice versa. These examples are perfect examples of what I like to call unstable senses of self. In other words, to identity disturbance.

That means you do not have a realistic understanding of believing yourself as far as who you indeed are as a person. To feel empty, to not know who you indeed are, filling in constant voids that don't have anything to do with you half of the time. But because your heart is as huge as it is, you decide to take those risks.

The loss of sense is not an excellent quality to have, but knowing its meaning is more than you will ever know. If you ever come across anything that has you feeling like you're alone, try not ever to hesitate and sit back before you answer yourself. And try coming to common ground when it comes to your brainstorming and continuous thoughts about self-disturbance. You probably have a roadblock with things going forward, but you can apply this meaning of self-disturbance and share with those around you and have them go through the feelings and steps right along with you. It would help if you took risks within yourself and for those around you that also look up to you as the person you are with the personality to spare.

There's so much out there to help someone to reach higher than their desired expectations. And to become disturbed is like allowing yourself to let you down. Honestly, there are no excuses why self-disturbance is such a huge ordeal. But you'd be surprised about how much people allow themselves to take on, and with the challenges you are brave enough to take on; it's relatively easy to lose yourself. Meanwhile, finding yourself is the best feeling overall in the world. If it is a good feeling, it will be an even better feeling for you. There's so much more out there than the things that we not only put ourselves through, but allow for ourselves to go through. There are probably some of you saying to yourself right now that you did not ask for the situation you're in, and that's completely understandable.

As I can relate to multiple topics and occasions, you can correct your outcome and give it a 180=degree turnaround. The meaning behind life is what you make of it is accurate and, without a doubt, there's so much out there. Rather than ponder over that one thing or situation.

It would help if you understood the differences between getting through and going through, because they sound similar. But when you think deeper in the mind, you will realize the difference. To get through, you must go through. Most people, including myself, know that I must get through, but I sometimes feel as if I am at a complete stopping point because of the many things that I go through.

It is your choice to determine whether or not the things you are going through are worth going through.

If you do something from your heart, you will never forget it. You must always give yourself that amount of credit and tell yourself that you come first. Your health, mentally, physically, and emotionally, plays a huge role in your outcome of getting through. You want to share your story as I can share mine and still move forward. To most, some things will never be good enough, and something they see is too good to be true. But there are those who know the vision and need that extra word of mouth, that extra boost.

Those are the people I am talking to, and I appreciate the time and patience dedicated to reading this book. If you ever find yourself being in a situation that leads to you being self-disturbed, try your best to refrain from the problem. Usually, someone typically gets stuck and continuously looks for that way out.

I do not see myself in everyone. I know the difference between those who are okay with getting by and those who have a voice. You never judge a book by its cover. But, it would help if you allowed people to speak their truths. Because in most cases you will hear what you've never known. There's so much that haunts people. when it comes to being disturbed;

I believe that you must know what energy to use, and if using any power is even in the question. There's so much behind self-disturbance that could keep your mind on a mission. It is how you decide to take the lead.

The energy that self-guidance holds can be like playing with fire in a sense and then again being as cold as ice if you can manage it right. I tell myself this all the time when it comes to self-disturbance. Now, in this time of my life, I'm not as bothered by many things that have bothered me so quickly before. Now I'm older, I have more experiences and ways of thinking and most certainty over my likes, dislikes, and so on. So yes, I allow things to add until they cannot add up anymore, but I pick and choose my battles, and not everything needs a response at that given time.

Some things need a response right then and there with no questions asked, no hesitation at all. But you will know when and when not to say something. You even know how to react or not to react. The act of self-disturbance is one of the essential qualities you could ever have that nobody can ever take away from you. This entire book helps guide you through the multiple stages of what it takes to become a better self within yourself.

I've realized that most of the things that we as people go through, we've either been put in or placed ourselves in the position, but are not set for success on ways to get out of the situations.

I look at it as there is always a way out and even more room for cleanup. By saying there is even more room for cleanup means that you can always do better. No matter what the situation is, due to it being your own decisions or caused by someone else, you can get up and out. And remain stable with this mental process. To use these steps of self will continue to get you through every single one of those moments that used always to seem somewhat impossible, when it is all possible. I believe that there is and will always be a way out—the challenges only bring a better you. To have no experience at all is like never learning.

How would one lead by example or share examples if they have never had to be that example physically? If you are going through things in your life right now that are putting you in discomfort, eliminate them slowly but surely. In some cases, you will probably eliminate certain situations quicker than others. This aims to place the things of importance in front of you. At the same time, the things that slow you down remain nonexistent or just behind you in the race.

Challenge your mind, and not one who seems only to belittle you or has nothing to bring to the table when it comes to your growth. But, of course, you do not want to become an entitled person. When someone feels entitled, it says that someone is obligated to do this or that for you, almost as if the world revolves only around you. As if you are this privileged human being.

It is okay to feel like you have control or even want control of something when it comes to how you may like certain things.

I want you to make sure that you understand everything there is to know when it comes to this characteristic of being self-disturbed and asking yourself what things or situations are going on in my life, whether it's right now, or times before that still come and go until this day. What are some challenges that I still face, whether within myself or others, that maybe if I'd either let go or had just let go - would those specific outcomes play a part in my now if it weren't for them? Sit back and think about the disturbances you have probably had and think about what could have been different. There's so much to ask yourself when it comes to evaluating. Most of the revaluation goes for someone else, or maybe I should say towards someone else, rather than within yourself and for yourself. So, this is a time to get back into your head. To have the type of thought process without allowing anyone or anything to overcome that in any sense. So many of us, including myself, never used to think that we needed any form of evaluation. But that is like saying that I am perfect, and nobody is perfect. It is not the situations you go through but how you accomplish them. I have learned that the hard way.

Meanwhile, now situations are put way more at ease by the level of discipline I have grown to have within myself to manage these situations. It is okay not to have the last word each time. And it's okay not to debate when something is said when you disagree. For you to allow someone to vent and you open your ears. Better yet, open your mind to hearing new situations, new things, new ways that you probably never even thought of or even gave the chance to listen to. To listen to what someone else is saying and find a positive within it, instead of just disagreeing or having your one-sided version of it all. This will begin to eliminate the burden on self-disturbances.

Think about the many things that you have been disturbed by. Is it that bad? Did it even have to be that bad? Have you had your self-disturbing check? And are you genuinely self-disturbed by someone else or your own well-being? Are you in a situation where you are happy? Where you are at peace, you will feel so much ease that you will be so in tune within yourself. If that is the case, then many people around you and situations you go through will not influence you easily, because you are your influencer and those around you.

Have you ever thought that maybe if you changed your well-being, those around you would reflect right off you? What if you are that buoyant energy ball that person must look up to and, better yet, the energy that others feed off? It's not about just you all the time, and most of the time, it just takes you fixing yourself to fix multiple people around you beginning.

It will then leave you to think, "Wow, all of this wasn't even that bad." Take out the time for once and abide by what made you happy. An influencer is what you want to be - that will help knock off the many self-disturbances you find yourself coming across, no matter how big or small. No challenge is a challenge when you have all the tools and the resources to maintain them.

There are influencers all around you, whether you

know it or not. Those influencers are making something out of nothing and turning it into money. Influence is much easier to control, which means that you are doing absolutely nothing, and to entertain bad results is not the route we're going to take in this book. It is all about the way up and how to get out. I want you to think about the word influence, and what it means to you, because you have reasonable and then you have bad, but we mainly apply it to something when we say, "Bad influence," leaving us to think and attach it to something that isn't good rather than lifting us to gain thought of the word "influencer."

Many words mean more than one thing, but we mainly hear people apply them to things when they are not good. So instead of complimenting and allowing that person to listen to that, the same word has an opposite that you could use positively. Some will share those words with you in an act. And in some cases, you will have to go and read them for yourself, or you get stuck with that word and how it was used and applied to you. You did not do or should have done something rather than what you did do.

Because self-disturbances are a challenge that we all face and have faced, some more than others; it could be exceedingly tricky reading this. I know I still go through challenges because we live this thing called life. But you will learn how to get through, especially after taking the keys of this book as your self-guidance and applying them when you have hit that patch where self-disturbance comes knocking right at your door.

You will then know how to answer it instead of just closing it, leaving another one to open.

Keep yourself within yourself, and do not let anyone take that creative piece away from you. For some, you do not have to change. Because you are who you are but know there is and will always be a time and a place to change if you want, but that's up to you to decide. I only give you the tools to overcome all these things. But never do I tell a person not to be themselves. In many situations, tests will continue throughout your life.

- **How will you ace your next test? Are you going to let the test run you, or are you going to take the test?"**
- **If someone tries to question you or your thought process to address it, how would you respond?**
- **Are you going to go by your old ways where nothing seemed to have worked or even change?**

You were steadily trying to beat the same horse with no outcome. Besides, you keep getting knocked back into space, leaving yourself with no room to follow. You do not want to ask yourself any of these questions and not know how to answer them or even act upon them. I want to do yourself a favor and remember this last part in this chapter to confirm that self-disturbance can go on and on.

There's no stopping point when it comes to examples. But there is a stopping point regarding what's going to be accepted. You will be much better off letting go of some things rather than just holding on.

I want everyone to find themselves again and start doing things that put that smile on their face. To realize that material things and people are not your only promises to happiness. It begins with you and within yourself. To have all those things in the world and still be self-disturbed means you have nothing at all. If that is the case, then you'll remain miserable. It's not saying don't have nice things, don't do nice things, but focus on what is worth having. What is having someone or something in your corner that is not there and that only contains a temporary placement with no guarantee? That is like having a life with no insurance. As we get older, we need security; I know I do.

To have a guarantee is practically an unconditional commitment. Knowing and believing that something is what it will be, whether it is good, or bad negative or positive, is just the all-around fact of knowing for sure about something instead of having those continuous what-ifs and overall uncertainties about something. Believe that whatever it is will have a meaning about it, and you will not leave yourself in the dust.

This book, of course, is a positive one, so I would hope the situations, whether adverse or harmful, will go towards the growth of good and positive for the better within yourself. Because this is all-important to guarantee something – it is an overall win in most cases because it allows you to have a chance at something. It allows one to take a risk while challenging what could be a win-lose situation, but, in this case, it is a win for the guarantee at the end of the race.

I had to think to myself if, with the amount of time spent and effort put into something, will my outcome be as profitable as the income I've put into all of this? And does it all balance out in the end, as a product of my environment? I have grown, and I feel good to have gone through a couple of the milestones that I have been through, and I am coming out with a better head up. I'm ahead of myself and there are times where I have to bring myself back down to reality, but it doesn't mean that it's impossible. It just means being realistic with yourself for the time being without going over your head.

JOURNAL

SELF-DISTURBANCE

BEFORE reading the chapter.

1. What does self-disturbance mean to you?

_____

_____

_____

_____

_____

_____

2. What characteristics does someone hold who carries the qualities of someone who's self-disturbed?

_____

_____

_____

_____

_____

_____

3. Do you consider yourself to be a person who follows the characteristics of being self-disturbed? If so, why or why not?

_____

_____

_____

_____

_____

_____

4. What is something that you have to learn when it comes to self-disturbance?

_____

_____

_____

_____

_____

_____

5. What personal strengths do you have when it comes to controlling things that could make you self-disturbed? And how do you grasp control?

_____

_____

_____

_____

_____

_____

AFTER reading the chapter.

1. What does self-disturbance mean after reading about it?

_____

_____

_____

_____

_____

_____

2. Do the same qualities apply that you suggested should be the qualities of someone who considers themself as someone who's self-disturbed, or have your examples of the qualities changed?

_____

_____

_____

_____

_____

_____

3. Depending on your response before reading the chapter. Do you either still consider or not consider yourself to be self-disturbed ?

_____

_____

_____

_____

_____

_____

4. What is something that sparks your interest that you'd

love to learn when it comes to handling yourself and self-disturbances?

_____

_____

_____

_____

_____

_____

5. What are a few of your favorite self-care activities? If you don't have any, then what are a few that you'd like to consider?

_____

_____

_____

_____

_____

_____

CHAPTER 6:

DISCREPANCIES

"Stop trying to force situations, whether it's out of something or somebody! Don't set expectations for something to happen that isn't in the position to happen. Nor can you allow something to happen if the timing isn't right; the conditions won't even allow it to happen. Not everything is going to please you or the next person. So take sensible directions. If you're willing to compromise, then that's a bonus. But first, ask yourself to what extent you feel and to which extent is beneficial for my own sake to help another in their situation beneficially."

-INicole Royce

There are lines between self and discrepancies. The combination of the two stands for how one applies this characteristic to yourself. It's the lack of ability to do something you might not get credit for, no matter how big or small. The word discrepancy shows a characteristic of inconsistency, and while applying it within could mean the amount of inconsistency that you lack within yourself. All of this could be a strength for some, but a weakness within others.

- When one thinks of themselves, how do they interpret it?
- What are some of the mighty pros and cons of

someone applying the meaning of self-discrepancies within their inner person?
- **How does all this influence you?**

To each his own, but to have such characteristics isn't the route you'll want to take; it's one you should wish to gain from along the way and with the many lessons taught and learned along your journey of life. Of course, this book helps guide effective daily ways of thinking that most people have to second-guess. The things that we believe are so common, yet so uncommon. The situations that we feel like we're able to address the same as the next and yet not fully grasp the understanding of such or the lending ear needed without a voice of reaction. The things that trigger us and that uplift us. The mix between the two things which tells you either you should or should not.

Meanwhile, all these things are what lead to one's discrepancies and, as I would like to call it, "self-discrepancies." Many people probably think that it means differences between or amongst something to explain the word discrepancy further. On the contrary, to have the difference between something or something else helps gain the qualities of being uniquely different within yourself. And the word discrepancy is the inconstancy of something, which are both two completely different settlements when it comes to abiding by yourself. Whether in similarity or compatibility, it lacks two or more things that should be alike.

Think with a Conscious Mind

I love to talk about discrepancies and how they are the perfect example of people continuing to understand themselves. This word plays a massive role in entitlement, and you do not even know it. You don't honestly know how much power overall this one word has with any situation amongst humans, but it's a part of our everyday lives. It will always find its way around uncertainty. Once you truly know yourself and have a mindful mind state, where no one or anything can ever take that away from you, then we are talking. But until then, there will always be room for discrepancies, whether low, medium, or high volume. It is the regular life cycle because nothing is perfect, of course.

Although it would be amazingly fantastic to live in a perfect world, would it really? If you have an ideal world without discrepancies, where is the balance? Discrepancies within yourself are the topic of this piece. I want to talk about this in a meaningful way that will touch your mind and expand your horizons of thoughts the way that your thought process grasps the attention of you and others. If we had the perfect world, it would not work, but there is a place for balance.

Be different and not indifferent. Have your opinions and have another as well. All of these things come into the topic of relations or relationships. Whatever the case, maybe it could even be a friendship, but all in all communication plays a huge role. I will use the example of two or more things that share similarities yet are comparable and should be alike, but are different.

All of this goes to speak for situations, arguments, disagreements that blow out of proportion that probably didn't even have to have the outcome they did, but yet we don't think about the result until its impacts are negative. That's when it hits, but what about before it gets to that negative point? Have you ever just stopped thinking and realizing how many times something negative will take a turn for the worse when everything is already going downhill? Better yet, how many times will a positive take a turn at its most high?

Meanwhile, we're unable to appreciate and gain positive peace because we're still overheated. And the negative has a brutal hit of an impact because we were so beat up about the thought process that we place ourselves in the predicament of allowing ourselves to get so out of character, and have not gained complete control over our thought process. We become overwhelmed, leaving ourselves to push something away, lose ourselves, or look for something else entirely in the process. It shouldn't get to that point; you should never say things without a proper thought process. Silence speaks more volumes than the number of words ever will, and is the key to a positive foundation. That's not to say that everything is nor will things ever be perfect. Still, every situation's outcome will be much easier to take every time, whether it's something minor or unfortunately tragic and life-changing.

Intuit Life Cycles

Your intake and overall mental state of discrepancies will help you realize which battles to fight and let go of. Have you ever been in a situation where you regret saying things that you, of course, probably shouldn't have ever said? Yet, it continues to hinder you at times and in ways that you'd never even start to believe? And sometimes, you wonder something so big or small could've been defused. If there was just that one peace of mind that thought it all through, without allowing the pure pressure of a situation to get you out of character. I love to use the example of friendship - you live, and you learn. Most of you ask me if some people that are considered your friend or acquaintance are placed into your life for the season for every reason.

I do believe the same goes for relationships as well that either are not doing so well or as great as they feel they should be doing, leaving nothing but animosity and discomfort, which there should never be. You'll without a doubt have your ups and downs in your agreements, but there should never be a thin line between the exchange of words or action.

There should never be a burn between the two during an altercation, and it should truly never be an altercation, just a former exchange of words, maybe a disagreement, but never something worth regret. Knowing yourself plays a huge role in how you treat others, and sometimes it takes that one person to help the other find themselves and lead the way, but both cannot do so while yelling. I thought about a saying one day that I voiced out loud after making up in my head while conversing with a previous employee at my job while working at Target, and I told them, "If you're both arguing, then who's really listening?"

By saying that, it opened ears to some, and their attention was probably caught later down the line. I personally feel like that quote that I created in my head was led by the example of previous examples set and made by myself that I've learned to grow from and grow with along the way. I take a lot of my life-learned lessons with me and abide by them. Another life example that I'd like to use is our coworkers, your colleagues, bosses, managers, whatever you call them; we have our discrepancies amongst everyone in that ballpark, but yet we're all here for the same reason and are looking to meet the same plan when it comes to the work environment and the finish line that we're trying to encounter within the company.

I am not talking about where we see ourselves personally but where we are for the time being, and to belittle someone instead of putting your heads together is never the key. The discrepancy within that example is two colleagues who share the same similarities and compatibility within things, topics, and situations within the workforce, but can't seem to come to a means with anything; instead, they insist on belittling one another without actually building.

The theory of self-discrepancies goes far deeper: social anxiety and depression are two main discrepancies that those around us, even yourself as your own being, might fail to overcome, and yet you're trying to figure out the way and find the actual means to overcoming your own personal discrepancies.

Those are two of the main problems and overall issues that many people, including myself, have experienced or are still experiencing and yet don't know what another way to overcome the feeling other than feeling as if there's no way out.

Have No Fear

There is always a way out. There is a way out for any challenge; it is all in your mind, and it has a lot to do with your destiny. Some people have never been forced or put in the situation to believe themselves while trying to motivate themselves through the challenges of life they seek to overcome. So not only has one not been tested to their fullest physically, but have you mentally? What do I mean by that exactly? To most thinking in the plane state of mind, it sounds like I'm saying that you haven't tried, but it's deeper than this. When I say, "Not only had one not tried to their fullest physically, but have you mentally?" You can try the physical all day long; every minute, second to the hour. But if your mind is not entirely there within the journey of your absence, what exactly have you overcome?

How many times have you, have we as people, including myself, tried to knock down a brick wall and jumped hurdle after hurdle, trying to either find a way or make a way out of what at the time may seem to be no way? But yet you wear yourself out physically and cannot think clearly. If only you'd sit back, relax, and process it all, you wouldn't have worn yourself out to the max with your physical wellbeing.

That is what causes one's depression and falls in place of overall anxiety within each one of us. It is the phycology of life, but it is how you withhold it. It's how you interpret and inherit what you take in when you receive the information. Do you take it all in at once? Do you grasp it, let it sink in, and then dominate? Or are you someone who takes what you can take and just run headfirst with the first bit of information that ion have and then point the finger to blame one for a decision or choice that you have every bit of importance in to include whatever it is that you felt the need to be included?

The meaning behind self-discrepancies goes far; it is almost too far in the mind of most. It's is more than just what it sounds and how it's interpreted. You never honestly think about the guidance that self-discrepancies have on either you or those around you. And its overall effect on understanding and being within the reasoning of their everyday life. You realize that you have complete control and, nonetheless, your sense of empowerment if you sit back. To observe more than you speak and analyze before your quickness to over-analyze, and then you're stuck having to fix another hole that you've opened up all because of either your misjudgment and sense of understanding when the only source is you. It starts with you and only you.

As soon as we understand ourselves as who we are, the better we'll be able to grasp others' attention in a more positive influence than just being heard; you'll have those around you listening. There's a difference. Let us start by asking yourself now if you have read the meaning behind the discrepancy. I have been in continuous situations where I have found myself learning as if I would never get it eventually, and turned my upside-downs right side up. I have been that person continuing and still, until this very day, a person who experiences discrepancies. There's a difference between continuous discrepancies and one whose learning from their discrepancies does not allow endless identical situations.

Differences between Impulsive and Concrete

You do not want your deprecatory actions to start becoming compulsive. The examples that I can truly stand by when it comes to my experiences of how I apply self-discrepancies to life and the daily challenges that I face consist of: dedication, determination, not taking on more than I can chew - as in not trying to handle more than my mind will allow for me to handle. To only take action towards things that are of value to my energy and the sake of others. To not only be able to set a positive example for me, but those around me. It is quite easy to carry on with your daily life, thinking of all the things you wish to achieve and accomplish. But it is also effortless not to follow those wishes you give yourself and then beat yourself up mentally because the outcome was not the same as you expected it to be.

There have been times where I had to reset my entire trend of thinking and the way of life towards the path that I wished to follow, whether that meant maintaining myself a little more than needed, or distancing myself from those who had no interest in not only their own interests or mine. Those who are unwilling to take the clear roads with you when it comes to powering one another and enduring your dreams, no matter what level of entry you are starting from. I have learned to realize that everyone must start somewhere, and having this characteristic is one that completely must change for the better if you wish to seek things differently.

I'm sure some things are going on right now in your life that you're abiding by; but then your actions take place, and you do another or possibly even say one thing, and yet you're not following up on your word or even admitting or taking ownership and overall accountability for something that was either done or stated. There are so many different formalities of the word discrepancy, and you will figure out where you stand the more you read. The characteristics of discrepancies that could help you determine where you stand are Opened, Ignored, Identified, Implemented, Not Implemented, and Failed. This breaks down the different discrepancy types for how one's mind thinks before deciding to turn around in either the wrong direction or the right, leaving them uncertain and inconsistent.

The first type of discrepancy is "opened." It is basically stating that when something is given or told to you, that you are open to it and willing to see what it is all about. Because something is fresh, you'll either be interested or uninterested, but still bothered by whatever it is. You then have the two choices of identifying or ignoring something. To identify would be looking into or being prone to hearing more about whatever it is acknowledged, and open to hearing or investigating more about whether you ask someone or look up the information yourself. In other words, to be interested in something. When you ignore it, that is another status of the lifecycle of discrepancies.

This means you are not interested and have no cares in the world about it, whether it is just for that given moment or a permanent decision of choice. After all these steps, you then have processed or failed. If you processed the information, it could either be good or bad. It could even result in action; negative and positive.

Meanwhile, you then have failed, which is just the same as ignored; you have no interest whatsoever, and your thoughts are the way of all thoughts. And that nothing anyone does or says could result in you changing your sense of opinion. To overcome a discrepancy can be rather tricky if your mental space is not in the right mind frame, and if your examples to lead are not positive ones. To believe that most thoughts that people have and speaking from myself of experience have to come from someone who cannot only tell you what you're lacking and have lacked, but compare their stories to ones of your own. To not make one feel as though he or she is at fault and alone in the situation. Giving examples allows a person to get a physical outlook on the conditions and visualize the problems they face. For many such as me, this was happening before I even knew that discrepancies were something that I was facing.

I never utterly understood what it was that I was doing wrong. I never understood what kept me holding back, and it turned out I was holding myself back because I had all the tools and resources without realizing it. Sometimes we face challenges that we don't always have to be in, but or stubbornness can dig a deeper hole for us than the one we'd rather be in, and we want to climb out of it and make it all disappear. How many times do you find yourself in a situation that you feel like you want to be rescued from, and then you come back into reality, and then you're upset at the world because it felt like your dream was so real? But it was not by a long shot and there is nothing you feel you can do about it, so you pressure yourself into believing something that is far from true. You probably sell yourself temporary forevers instead of being completely honest and true to not those around you, but you.

To be true to those around you; yes, that is the genuine guideline. But being true to yourself and disciplining your mind to believe, and abiding by and achieving your commands and demands are most important. The moment you give yourself that same respect and recognition, and most of all, patience to believe yourself and your capabilities, you will no longer feel as though you must cover up lies anymore, which I call extended stories. And as I have stated before, temporary forevers.

Don't pretend to live a life that you don't wish to live instead of seeking betterment within the one you now live. This topic can be overly sensitive to most, because there is a lot of self-work put into place. Each person has their own interpretations of the meaning of something, and the examples that you lead by may be viewed differently in the eyes of someone else.

It is not so much of what you say or how something is said, but how you interpret it. To have a complete understanding and grasp of the meaning is what is most important. I believe that everyone is entitled to their opinions, but it is still good to help lead the way if possible to find at least the track where they'd wish to be. Sometimes it takes that extra boost that's needed for someone to, if not see it for themselves, hear it from someone, but for some, they can be told the same thing over and over again, and it just does not register.

Sometimes, it takes those on the outside to tell you exactly what you've heard on the inside. Still, because it comes from an outside source, the meaning then applies differently and more forcefully, allowing the person to grasp and understand. After not understanding, you realize that certain consequences come with everything, both good and bad. This takes quite a bit of time sometimes. To find the you that you're destined to be and, better yet, not to have to constantly be reminded of who you are and the dreams you plan to pursue to ensure that you become an even better you. The discrepancy of one thing over another can go on and on; that is when you must pick and choose your battles.

There will forever be discrepancies, as many continue to be more and more challenging in our life every day. But how do we go about them, and how do we abide by the situations that could overcome us if only we allowed them to? Not many people know the difference between discrepancy and differences, and they seem to be quite similar. To be different is to compare or contrast one thing over another and point out the dissimilarities.

In contrast, discrepancies hold a fairground between comparability and similarities. In most cases, it's inconstancies, differences, disparities, or multiple disagreements about something. The word discrepancy has more to do with the sentiments and overall facts that something holds representation over with more meaning supporting its argument.

This chapter is focused on your self-discrepancies, the differences you have, and understanding the discrepancy of the argument or disagreements besides leaving it to be just one-sided. Do you find yourself losing the level or overall amount of balance between yourself or someone else when having a dispute, or just a conversation of trying to figure something out? And does it go right, or does it take a turn in the left direction while you're trying to analyze the problem? In some circumstances, the problem is not when they are too much different, but when the situations or things are too much alike. But we do not often see that type of discrepancy because they were already so stuck in the mind frame of who is right over the other, instead of insisting on analyzing how both ideas could come together.

This leads to developing the start of a discrepancy - keep in mind discrepancies are not bad.

When I was introduced to these word discrepancies. I took the word as a negative, meaning I did not think I could apply it to anything good. I automatically thought that discrepancies meant an argument, something that took a turn for the left instead of what I would say in "the right direction." Why did I take it in that context? Because I was not properly given the meaning of anything positive behind the word. When you do not know what something means, it's best to look it up, and while using the word, it's best not always to use it in a negative while in communication with someone.

To me, this word discrepancies was very one-sided. The word and its meaning hold a bigger meaning for me, so I decided to make it a chapter in the book. I feel it is a word of importance and a word that we fail to listen to as closely as it's interpreted while in a sentence. And if misused, its natural meaning will go forgotten.

I could have dodged many bullets if only I had known what I know now. This leads me to look in no other direction but forward. I also apply things that have made me who I am today in others' thoughts and minds. When something is not so good, there is always a positive that comes out of it.

However, you might not see it right away, but your assurance of knowing means you can continue to remain at your most positive by doing your part instead of just talking about it. We hope all day for the best in something and the best within things, including those around us and ourselves, but are we putting ourselves in the position to succeed and notice those changes?

There comes a time where you must sit yourself down and re-evaluate time and time again because you will never be for sure. But one thing is for certain - when you know, you will know. The word discrepancy can hold many people back and block out a lot of pride that you thought you had if not handled with care. Whether it's towards others or words that have been used towards us, the words that we regularly use can truly make or break us.

We should be mindful and aware of the power behind words that we use. I want you to think about the word discrepancy and think about the word different. I want you to remember the meanings that you had about the two words.

Afterward, I want you to think of the new meaning that you now have about the two. Try coming to peace with the new meaning, and you will soon feel your mind turning to a different side. At times, you don't notice certain things until someone else points it out to you or until you've been through a life-changing experience that causes you to correct yourself. And those are directions that we do not want to face.

But whether it is secret or brought to light, you know how to find your calm within this as I have learned to find mine. No matter the situation, these steps of discrepancies and the passage of this entire book will lead you to grow in many directions - more than what you ever wished to imagine - and your mind will thank you later. Let us get to avoiding these discrepancies that could get in your way before it even happens. It is sort of like looking into your intuition.

This is nothing to do with the intentions of you being a psychic or saying that you're going to know each and everything before it happens; it's more so along the lines of common practices of avoiding situations by simply doing things you should be doing to protect yourself, your mind, and your own mental headspace. These things typically include being in tune with the situations and observing them, such as how often it is happening, if that someone is doing all in their might to change or fix the issue. Suppose the same energy given by you yourself is the same energy being applied by someone with the situation, causing you to come to the rescue each time.

Also, place yourself around those with the same similarities, those who you can grow from. Bring to the table just as much as you possibly give, and feel as if you are valued and appreciated for doing just that and then some. It is recognition for what you are doing instead of believing your thoughts and actions go unnoticed. I believe in also setting procedures throughout the process. Give yourself a chance to notice things before allowing yourself to go completely headfirst into something and leaving yourself with nothing but heartache in the long run.

Whether it's hindering you financially, mentally, or physically, leading you to deal with things, people, or situations that you could disregard if only you stopped allowing for it to happen. You have a point where you are about ready to break and let everyone know how you feel. Better yet, go ahead and nip it all in the bud at the very beginning, before anything is even allowed to happen. If you practically set all of your boundaries and foundations at the door for what you expected, you know the results if those requirements are not met.

Lastly, I believe in never sticking to only one way. No matter how much that one-way works, it has worked and is continuously working. I believe in always finding more ways to explore when it comes to investigating other ways out of your discrepancies. The situations you go through will always be different, no matter how much they may seem similar in some cases. In every situation, no matter how similar they may seem, you are always dealing with a different person, and not everyone can be addressed the same.

Have different ways of handling your discrepancies and overall situations. That is where most people mess up. Because there is a thin line between treating all people the same and thinking you can talk to anyone in any way. There's a level of respect for anything and any points you need to get across, but some fail because their points to one might not trigger the other person the same as they did the last.

You must be mindful and put yourself in the shoes of

the person and think to yourself, did you like it? Would you have liked that or would it have put you in defense mode if this were a situation? No matter how much of a point someone was trying to make, it is all a matter of how you say certain things and not always what you say. Although what you say can also be strategic. Being in tune with your intuition can get you out of a lot of situations that you'll begin to realize if handled differently you would've been out of it, avoiding unnecessary conflict. The situations probably could've either been avoided or easily corrected. What you say to people could also be strategic.

When you go through the process of elimination to situations that could happen, and you ask yourself, okay, if I do this, what is my outcome? And if this isn't done, what's the long-term effect that this could have, whether it's with me or whoever is complying? And of course, these are all thoughts that we think at times in the aftermath of everything or at its peak instead of in the beginning.

Because in the beginning, we were going off fresh emotion most of the time, and we say the first thought that comes to mind without simply analyzing. The moment we began to analyze our full thoughts is when the top peak comes. And by that time, it is too late because the peak can either take a positive turn or a negative, and it is your choice on how to level it down or bring it right back up. These are all roles of how we should do things, but do we ever truly do things the right way? And who can say that these ways are the right way? But of course, in my mind, these are the ways that have steered me right. Things that may steer things right for me might not steer another in the direction of the same.

Although, I am prone to sharing my thoughts and opinions that have helped and guide me. Who will truly make each person in this world happy? Nobody, no matter how right you are about something or how much sense something makes. There will forever be those select few that have to make a joke out of it or turn it into the most hateful thing possible.

And that's when you have to continue to pat yourself on the back because you know that you're touching everybody when you're hitting nerves by simply speaking the truth that you believe in, and ignoring the thoughts of others that aren't anything less than uplifting and overall self-motivating. If I were to sit back and worry about the things people thought over, I believe it wouldn't be helpful.

All of that would get me everywhere besides where I am destined to be. I will forever continue to share my thoughts and remain trying to lift people up with the insecurities they have, and try my best to turn them around and into the securities they will blossom to having. It is okay to have doubts, it is okay to have flaws, it is okay to stand out, and it is okay to have different mind frames. It is okay to have a different mind frame and yet still be open to hearing about others and their thoughts.

There is no exact way, and there is no right way to

lead someone to positive things when your interest is at its best. But there is a wrong way when you're negative and bringing negative vibrations along the way, and inviting that energy that is not needed or which will be accounted for if you continue to keep it up.

There's always room for positive in my eyes, and up-lifting motivation. At times, those who are most hurt continue to hurt others, but does that make it right? It does not make it right, but everyone needs guidance, whether you have had little to no guidance. And then you must keep in mind that some just cannot be guided, and they have to miss out on the wave if they're unable to join it. But with all of that comes patience, and with patience comes time. Because all we truly endure is time, but we have this world which continuously reminds us of all the time we have left. It is how you value your time and what you decide to do with that time; in my time, not only do I continue to work on myself, but I try my best to help others in the process.

I consider myself a role model and work in progress and an example to lead by when it comes to things being possible. And in my eyes, I believe for anything to be possible. Anyone who thinks differently, I try my best to lift them because this mind frame does not happen over time, but working out the nooks in mine helps me elevate others' problems. You must be in-tune with yourself as much as you are with someone else if you're the person that I'm speaking to, whether it's the person who's trying to help or the person who's genuinely crying out for help. There's room for everyone, and there is a place for guidance if you are willing to be guided. It starts with you; that is when you ask yourself if you are ready or willing. To be ready is one thing, because no one's truly ready for any circumstances and no matter how much you plan for things.

The way of life always has its ways to work it out in ways it feels is best, But you can be willing, and in the case of being willing means you're ready for whatever ball life throws. You will dodge the curveballs, and words that are anything other than captivating will end up going over your head. And you will continue to move right along as if nothing even phased you. This is the right direction; you will feel the vibrations with just that one motion of not being bothered. All of this is what I mean by being locked in within your own intuitions. When you are locked in with your own intuitions, nobody will be able to get to you.

The situations that had once upset you will begin only to make you laugh with sarcasm, because you know your patience was once limited and how you react would only be a setback. It will lead you to notice others' different movements and ways, leading you to study different body language that you once had and only remind you to see yourself within that someone else. And you will conclude that you either liked that way or did not, and you will choose your sense of direction from then on out. The direction I hope to see you choose is the most positive direction and only using your strength of retaliation as needed.

JOURNAL:
DISCREPANCIES

BEFORE reading the chapter

1. What does the word discrepancy mean to you?

_____

_____

_____

_____

_____

_____

2. What does it mean to have a discrepancy?

_____

_____

_____

_____

_____

_____

3. Talk about a time and/ or an experience where discrepancies have played a role in something you've done or either experienced, whether it was physical, mental, or an emotional state.

_____

_____

_____

_____

_____

4. Do you practice mindfulness in your everyday life?

_____

_____

_____

_____

_____

_____

5. Are you as a discipline as you'd like to be when it comes to discrepancies that may occur?

_____

_____

_____

_____

_____

_____

AFTER reading the chapter

1. After reading this chapter, does your meaning of discrepancies remain the same or indifferent from the answer you had before reading this chapter?

_____

_____

_____

_____

_____

_____

2. Do you feel as if after reading this chapter that you now have more control over the way discrepancies can have either a more positive or negative effect on your life?

_____
_____
_____
_____
_____
_____

3. Now that you have read the chapter. How would you share with someone your ideal thought for overcoming any form of discrepancies?

_____
_____
_____
_____
_____
_____

4. If someone else were to describe you, what do you think they'd say?

_____
_____
_____
_____
_____
_____

5.) If you had a brief moment of pause in front of an audi-
ence of people actually to hear you out. What would you
say when it comes to discrepancies that you've had to
come incompliant with?

_____

_____

_____

_____

_____

_____

CHAPTER 7
SELF-ABUNDANCE

"Don't take on more than you can handle in any given situation. Allow yourself to enjoy and actually grasp the meaning behind things and their value, rather than just having a collection of things, thoughts, people, or whatever strikes your attention. Let your mind rest and take things one step at a time. Please don't overdo it. Remember, consistency is key. The only time limit that you're on is with yourself."

-INicole Royce

Don't Take It For Granted

This is referring to the abundance within something and what it stands for, and the amount of appreciation it could hold. The abundance of quality or the many qualities. The self-gain of abundance and what it means behind the person of self. Have you once asked yourself if you have mastered this phase in your life? Do you know what self-abundance means? Or better yet, the word abundance within its own definition? The definition of abundance means a rather large quantity of something, or to have multiple of something.

I use the title of this chapter 'self-abundance' as one of importance behind the meaning of self, and I consider it to be a solid quality when it comes to one taking part in learning his or her self. I look at self-abundance as an important quality to have, because it allows you to have not only one, but multiple characteristics when it comes to balancing yourself.

Balancing self-abundance and how it not only applies to your everyday life, but to the importance that it holds within things that actually matter, vs. things that you've kept up with and followed through with that had no real meaning or addition to your life. I look at the meaning of self-abundance as being something that we ignore.

Meanwhile, we keep up with things that do us no justice or mean us no good. Further, we do not give ourselves the credit that is due. We lack our quality of self-abundance and give recognition towards things that do not matter vs. things that do. I look at the meaning behind the word "abundance" as being positively pure. In more instances than just one.

I believe having an abundance of something means to have multiple of; in other words, more than just something that you need but which you need to maintain that balance all across the board with wants and desires; being able to level everything out and not just to become one-sided but open to multiple things that could lead you to bigger and better. This instance refers to self, and part of "self-abundance" has a lot to do with learning you and your inner self, and by doing so, you'll be able to apply that feature to multiple qualities that will soon become your strength and your superpower.

The meaning behind the word abundance is something I believe in that brings value to something and which has more meaning towards whatever you believe in and strive towards. I like to bring up the two meanings that confuse some like the words power, abundance, and prosperity. It gets intense when putting these two words side by side or even speaking of the meaning behind both words and what they mean when in use. The word prosperity is more so in the meaning of the material; something that is materialistic. The opposite, which is abundance, is more so the return of value that something has in place of that material thing, whether it is a natural or supernatural being or thing.

This may all seem like one big circle, but I like to break down everything that I speak about in more broad ways than some and give a visual breakdown. Without meaning, there is no real understanding. First, you have abundance; it's natural and from the heart. It benefits your inner self, mind, body, and spirit; it includes things of such: love, peace, happiness, integrity, wisdom, gratitude, positivity, respect, and so much more = I could go on and on with the gain it brings to someone by having this one quality. When you have this quality of abundance, everything that's brought to you, everything that has something to do with you, everything that you see, hear, touch, feel any and everything that you become a part of, then becomes a part of you with a more positive effect - it has a positive gain on you 99.9% of the time vs. that which prosperity does.

Prosperity can sometimes let out the true colors in some people who don't truly stand by whatever they support from the heart. If someone gains prosperity over something that brings a return to value, it is, in other words, more prone to have more tangible dividends. You can have all of the physical things in touch - holding, driving, living all of the tangible things of living the dream - and still not feel nearly as much as you would from the quality of "abundance". Without that, what do you truly have if out of prosperity you're still not happy the phrase? Then comes about "money doesn't buy happiness" so on and so forth.

In other words, if something is genuine, you would be open to abundance and open to prosperity - but do not ever let it become who you are as a person. It's like wishing the best for something or someone but not becoming disappointed when your plan does not go as desired, or having the hopes set at an all-time high that you're unable to bring down because of your own personal pride. I tell everyone to continue to be yourself, to listen to yourself, and not to allow prosperity to define who you are as a person. With the type of world that we live in, the type of people we place ourselves around are ones we feel an entitlement, as though we can get anything out of them other than general wealth, popularity and clout.

If you keep belief within yourself, then self-abundance will suit you just fine, and you'll then only have yourself to justify - you won't have to feel as if you have anyone else you need to answer to because you're your only confirmation. To be positive and pure within yourself should be the only source of confirmation that you need. It's much easier said than done not to be upset about something, not to have doubts about something, and I wouldn't be human or myself if I told you that still wasn't me because I wouldn't be telling the truth. And the first step of growth is to be honest with those around and true to yourself.

This is just a stepping stone to continue to help those who are still in the quality phase of learning themselves and how to and not to go about it - if your way is what works for you, then so be it, and with all due respect abide by it, but never allow your quality and sense of direction that's not working out to well be the only sense of direction that you choose to grasp.

I advise everyone to be mindful and open to learning, open to listening, open to physically experiencing and experimenting. I don't lead by a lecture; I lead by example, and practice of experience is something that I truly stand by because. I'm walking proof that without this characteristic, you'll be stuck and remain in the hole that you're trying to get out of.

Loosen Up a Bit

You don't want to be stubborn and narrow-minded; open up your thoughts, broaden your horizons, your sense of thinking to get more profound. The ideas you have could all change. You have a sense of thinking; have you tried asking yourself if that same sense of thought will lead you to where you're trying to go, and not just where you are or trying to be? People must get out of their thinking that they are average, and think more profoundly than the average. I try to lead people in the direction of being better than you not only once were and could become, but better than you are now. Reading this and learning something new will lead you to the first step of becoming better today as you were yesterday, all by just following these simple steps.

I can't stress enough how much knowledge there is out there. And where it could all begin to flow and how smoothly it will come once you finally give yourself the actual credit that you need. That doesn't mean the amount of money you have, or better yet, what you have to show for it.

It simply starts with your mind and where you choose to take it; if you do not use the thoughts you have and challenge yourself in the process, those are just cells wasted. The thoughts that you have that you never use are there; they don't just disappear. I have to be reached; there has to be a reason you decide to challenge yourself more and more. Sometimes it takes that extra push. Before you know it, that push will all come naturally, and you will then train yourself, and your beliefs will become more open.

The way that you think, hear, speak, and say things will then venture out. You'll have all of your qualities and characteristics flowing in one setting where you'll all of a sudden be able to control each manageably, and every single thought without feeling under pressure and without feeling like that outsider that you probably feel. Instead, you'll dedicate that characteristic towards something positive while believing and abiding by what you actually stand for, because what you stand for is a representation of you in every which shape or form. So, with this chapter, I want you to continue to think about "self-abundance" and if you can apply it to your everyday life and sense of thinking.

I want you to ask yourself if you understand the meanings behind the word abundance and prosperity the way you felt you did, and if your thought is not the same after reading. I need for you to grasp the qualities of self-abundance and how much of an importance there is behind the meaning of finding and knowing your true character.

I want you to not only grasp understanding, but be able to admit and give yourself the credit of not knowing previously. This is a lesson to help towards growth, not to point any fingers or be judgmental, but to help lead as directed and guide where there is guidance. I'm open and willing to lead what I've come across and guide as to what helped me and the thought process that it took for me to build myself, along with following the actions you learn behind it. I look at the word abundance, and I continuously think of myself in ways that I never used to feel.

I have become more and more prone to abundance and realized how it has had a major impact on not only the life of me, but those around me as well. The abundance that I can share, leading up to the experience, is the amount of love I choose to give. The characteristics that I have and that nobody can ever take away from you. To have abundance means to have much more than needed while remaining humble at the same time. It could most likely be mistaken for selfish, but it is far from the meaning of selfish. This word has multiple meanings, such as excess, plenty, or wealth of something. And it can be divided into multiple situations and I'll split it into the most understandable way for you—a time where I have had to apply and manage self-abundance. I would be with a job, but have other things I would prefer doing.

Meanwhile, what I was doing ended up having more impact on me because I was focused on all the wrong things. But now I'm focused on the right path with my head on straight, and knowing that the jobs that I may be going to momentarily can still be filled and not hold such a negative impact on me. I go into these establishments of work, restaurants, and businesses with the mentality that I someday soon will be wearing the shoe that fits. The amount of knowledge you are given could play a huge role in the amount of self-abundance you give yourself. If you dream big and want bigger, then your dream has become a sneak peek of your reality, and you then have to live in disguise to protect your inner self, your ideas your overall plans.

I believe that each person is molded differently, of course, but we all have the brilliant mind state that we sometimes allow to go to waste, and we should not.

That should not be the case because we all must excel our minds into thinking that would typically be abnormal to anyone else's morality. I believe that someone should be able to open themselves up to engage more with their general feelings about not only giving abundance or showing self-abundance within, but opening yourself up to receiving abundance and knowing how to take in the delivery properly.

To open yourself up for a change when it comes to receiving abundance. The stages needed that I feel are most important are being able to stand clear and positive within your words and abide by the actions you share. To be direct about what you are either wanting to say or are continuously talking about at that moment. The next step to it all would be to claim your dream and overall desires. In other words to speak your ideas, dreams, and life goals into the existence of wanting plans to work out for yourself - and not just from or because of the urgency of others.

Although things that people say to you could help give you that extra boost, in most cases it's you not being as certain as you'd like to be when it comes to figuring out your own decisions and actually coming to a point in your life of certainty to where it's all clear. It will not be as easy to influence you or steer you in any other direction than your own . It is easy to be manipulated or for your thought process to shift when you are not completely on the track needed to overcome your achievements. I know for a fact, and from walking proof of my own inner obstacles, that you must go through. Going through, you must get through whatever it is that is keeping that continuous roadblock along your journey.

This thing called life is a rollercoaster and practically a vision in disguise. Any and everything is possible and more possible than impossible. But we place ourselves to believe sometimes that we're incapable of one situation. Meanwhile, we need all the uplift and motivation about our decisions when our own self and inner thoughts surround us. As people with anything you want to overcome, we must learn to love ourselves just as much as someone else does, or even love ourselves harder when someone else does not, following your dreams into existence.

Then you will be on track to imply your dreams within your day, and it will soon become a part of your day. I believe that you must apply your positives and the growth of what you want to do compared to what you are doing, and have a motivational pick me up along the way. Instead of complaining about what you're doing, I have learned to use those things.

For example, the job that you know you must go to in order to support you and your family. To quit is not the right answer. You will only stir yourself into a bigger pot than the one that is already boiling for you. Although you see things that offer residual income and ideas that people have, every story is not the same. The experiences that may lead to one may not lead to you the same when determining the outcome. I believe that everyone is open to the same amount of resources; it just depends on how you use them, and they are all around you. Believing in yourself with the self-abundance quality that is installed within you must be as simple as that.

The dreams and ambitions that you have given yourself are a test, and you can see if it is something that you want to do or if it is just a phase. You will soon realize that the time and energy are working or not for you. I know little by little, bit by bit, each day, my goal with writing my book and perusing the lifeline needed for me to become successful took risks and challenges face. But with anything that you do, you need to apply yourself just as hard with what you're doing to get by to support your realistic lifestyle; but also keep in mind the lifestyle where you're trying to be and remain investing just as much time into that, so that your balance is equal.

There have been times, which I'm sure you can relate as well, where I feel as if I'm struggling to get something done or have yet to apply myself the way that I knew that I probably should've applied myself. I see the timeline and the gaps between where I am and where I should be, and notice that if only I'd invested that same amount of not only time, but energy, in my life-long desire, and not so much into other businesses or goals towards helping someone else get rich, I'd probably be in the position I'd want to be in.

Instead of looking back and being disappointed at those around me and holding grudges and living in continuous thoughts of faults because I'm not where I want to be, taking it out on anyone or anything, I've learned and grounded myself more and more every day. The same problems and sacrifices that I've challenged myself into believing while following the actions that take place is what now allows me to reach out to those of you who decided to read my book and possibly apply it to your own lifestyle.

Captivating You Within Self

The ability to cultivate an attitude of gratitude is another step that will complete you within this journey of abundance. To begin, start by asking yourself what the word cultivate means, and how do I get the best of it? The word cultivate holds meaning amongst something that is being developed in the beginning stages of something, and allows one to prepare for that certain something that is being molded. The meaning of cultivating an attitude of gratitude means to be thankful for something, to show appreciation for the quality of kindness that is being given, whether it's from you, the deliverer, or the sender.

The abundance of self holds the quality of you being appreciative of yourself and reaching that step of preparing and building yourself for the future. To work yourself upwards and continuing to grow and reach the stars, as some would say. To put all the hard work and dedication into not only a visual, by word of mouth, but by actions, as words shall follow. To hold yourself accountable and realize that you can go as far as you allow for yourself to, and the sky is the limit. You'll learn to value not only those around you and things around you that you never valued or not once seemed interested in, but it'll also allows you to open and discover a different sense than you ever even thought you had.

160

As a person who worked hard and owned up to their flaws, you will begin to give yourself more credit where credit is due, and the amount of gratitude that you yourself know that you deserve. Sometimes we allow ourselves to get belittled, instead of gaining that certainty.

I'm a firm believer in the word gratitude for trying to get to a place in life mentally, physically, and spiritually to wherever degree you choose, within whatever route you decide to go. Having gratitude is most important because it allows you to open another side of you that not even you knew that you ever had. It allows you to share that positivity and that overall energy that you wished to someday spread and share within those around you.

But once you give yourself that extra push that you always needed, you will seek things through to be so much easier throughout your journey, and with fewer complaints come gifts. The gifts which you will begin to receive will be gifts that guide you and never to lie to you. You'll have the abilities for any information that you've allowed your mind to open up to ,and accept information and turn it into a motivational adventure of growth with that your wisdom will gain and never go to waste. You had no intentions of looking at those things as a waste of time but a milestone towards your growth, figuring out how you can apply it.

The perception of one seeking gratitude holds such a powerful encounter that not many people have and can actually hold on to. But once you have reached that level, there is nothing that anyone will be able to take away from you. The level of happiness you'll have will not go anywhere, and you'll be more cautious of who you allow entering into your positive peace and who you'll sit back and watch from a distance. The abundance of self falls in so many categories more than just one, and the steps that lead up to one having abundance for themselves is more than just something that comes overnight.

I can honestly say that along this journey of mine I have learned to gain nothing less than gratitude, and I am constantly reminded of this each time I write.

To be a positive impact is and has always been a goal of mine to conquer at its highest level. Meanwhile, it's naturally applied within my everyday life, whether I mean to come across a situation or not. I am always thankful for each situation that comes my way, because I feel I can make it better for someone else's as I have built for myself. To each its own, and everyone handles situations differently.

I believe that the steps can still work in a person's good favor, just the same as any other if you apply it as given. And this all falls in with the universe waiting to say yes. I love this meaning behind the universe accepting. It's only right that you began to accept, and then you allow those around you to build their trust and accept too. You will then get the respect of the universe, and the ball is in your hands. The moment you get the universe to accept is the day that you reach your highest. This is not saying that each person in the world will agree with you and like everything that you say or do. Nor is it saying that you will not face any challenges or have minor setbacks.

The meaning of the universe saying yes practically says that you've not only accepted the challenges that come with the hard work and dedication that you've put into something, but that you're willing to face the challenges and actually abide by them, giving it all that you've got. The things that come your way that try and hinder us won't be allowed to, and will go unnoticed because your overall vision is much bigger and more vivid than allowing something minor to affect the big picture you've painted and have worked so hard for. The universe then has no choice but to respect your craft by allowing it to stand for what it stands for, because of the abundance within yourself that you have molded into believing.

Once you believe within yourself, then everyone else will follow. But until you allow yourself to have that same amount of energy that you put into things which have no interest in your own physical well-being and self-growth, you will never utterly understand. And I have learned the meaning behind the saying: "How do you expect someone else to believe you when you don't even believe yourself?" This is very much so factual, and there is a time and place for everything. You can be doing the same thing that you have been doing for years, and it still does not work out for you. The timing may have been off, or you might have just not had the knowledge needed to move on to the next level. I sure hope this meaning of self-abundance has helped you and will help you continue to be uplifted and self-motivated.

As we all should remember, you are your own motivation. There are things out there that could help make the
decisions easier. Things that could give you all the answers you need to know, and a sense of direction that need
to be taken. But seriously, are you not ready to apply any
of that yourself without a push from someone else?

To lead by example is the number one thing that I am
always surprised by. To be an example of what you stand
for is how you should direct. Don't do something or go in
a direction that doesn't make sense to you or if you're not
sure exactly why you're going in that direction. Never allow yourself to be pressured into a situation that you will
not be able to get out of. Always make sure that you can
protect yourself no matter the circumstance. Nobody else
is in your corner, although everybody needs somebody.
Never allow yourself to be in any situation without being
prepared, or at least have plans behind the outcome.
There's always a way out if there is a way into something.
Be your leading self-guidance even when a positive figure
is ahead of you.

Hold accountability within yourself and abide by everything you as a person within yourself love. Be that perfectly imperfect example of someone who never lets up.
You'll begin to feel that change and quickly start noticing
people who aren't in the position to go with you, but are
those who'll either watch on the sidelines or slowly meet
you at the finish line and match up with you later. And
then you have those who are not right there where you
have grown, and everything is not for everybody.

I believe that there comes balance with life, and you need each situation to help balance out a circumstance, but never should you want anyone to fail. There's nothing easy worth fighting for.

The ones who easily get things handed to them are the ones who typically don't know how to play all across the board when it comes to both book and street smarts, but you have to have the balance of both. There's the game of life you live and the game of life that you play, and it's up for you to choose the one you'd rather seek a future.

JOURNAL
SELF-ABUNDANCE

BEFORE reading the chapter.

1. What is self abundance?

_____
_____
_____
_____
_____
_____

2. What is an example of what the word self abundance means to you?

_____
_____
_____
_____
_____
_____

3. What have you dealt with in life that complies with using the characteristic of self-abundance?

_____
_____
_____
_____
_____
_____

4. How many people do you genuinely have in your inner circle?

_____
_____
_____
_____
_____
_____

5. What characteristic out of self-abundance after reading do you feel is a good characteristic to have?

_____
_____
_____
_____
_____
_____

AFTER reading the chapter.

1. Does the meaning of self-abundance remain the same now that you've read the chapter than before reading the chapter?

_____
_____
_____
_____
_____
_____

2. Who's someone you've always looked at as being your role model in life? What characteristics did he or she have that made this your person of choice?

_____
_____
_____
_____
_____
_____

3. Share something about this chapter after reading that has you excited?

_____
_____
_____
_____
_____
_____

4. Share something that you struggle with about "self abundance".

_____
_____
_____
_____
_____
_____

5. How often did you practice self abundance?

_____
_____
_____
_____

CHAPTER 8
SELF-SACRIFICE

"You should consider putting yourself first for once. Try your best to eliminate any and every distraction preventable. You will feed into some things, and some are not worth investing in at all. Remember to pick and choose wisely because that one move might knock your blocks down, leaving you to build back up instead of just filling in the blanks. Sometimes you're placed in situations to determine the outcome of your situation. Remember that everything that you do has a purpose and meaning behind it. No matter how big or small, effortless or endless that you think it might be. To every situation there's a meaning, and to every situation, there's a consequence. Not all consequences are bad ones."

-INicole Royce

The movement is beyond everything and everyone—the peace between wanting yourself and loving yourself—the equilibrium between admiring your desire and owning what you've seen before. Look at the momentum of what you wished; was maybe wondered what if, but which could now actually become a glimpse of what seeks to appear as your reality. The belief that you have always withheld but never held when exposed. You should reveal your thoughts and determine what matters most to you.

The question of what exactly is self-sacrifice? And the meaning within the words.

There is a vast difference between knowing what the word self means and knowing how to use the word. It sounds effortless to say, but do you truly understand what the abiding meaning of self means other than just having the response to be "you"? The true abiding sense of the word self is someone of their individuality, held account-able within their reflections and consequences.

When someone represents their individuality as a per-son, and is someone who is not trying to be someone other than themselves with their sense of belief and overall character, it makes them unique. It gets intense when talk-ing to someone about self and the different types of self that lead to who you will become. You have the first ideal of self-known as your ego, you have your superficial self of mind over body, and then you have your true self, the real you.

I believe that all these self-characteristics have their ways of being discovered; we see them each day. How-ever, some actions take the place of these characteristics that lead to people making first impressions, getting a sec-ond chance, or even being misjudged or judged off of the uncertainty that they continuously deliver based on the messages they give off.

Many of us hear the word ego all the time, and we automatically think negatively. But is the word ego indeed a negative thing to have, if it is one of three characteristics that each individual holds?

What does the word ego genuinely mean, and what is it? To have a big ego means to gain a sense of self-esteem or minor importance. To some, this could be beneficial, and to some, it could most definitely go over their heads and take a turn for the worse. In most cases, you need you to need for your self-esteem to have a boost.

The ego is a part of both your conscious and unconscious mind. And we should decide which of these to use while doing so. We do not often think in our most conscious minds when the ego becomes worse in believing and understanding its meaning. You hardly ever see anyone who positively boosts this word, so you fail to understand the value of the true purpose which it holds. There are different egos that I believe are worth criticizing.

Some love the thought of having an 'ego' or the enjoyment of the temporary feeling of being in charge or, as I'd like to say, a boss. To develop your ego means to believe in yourself, and trust the dedication and abidance that you give yourself within.

Trust in the steps you take and believe that the dedication you put into something worth creating or worth building, even worth crossing your mind, is crucial and plays a massive role in your success. I recognized the second example of the three self-identity identities that I recalled is your superficial self. What is one's shallow self? The meaning behind external self is when someone is, for example, "too good to be true." This is a well-known phrase that we have all heard before. Your superficial self is of uncertainty, someone you believe you are, but you have not yet reached that point. Someone who is thinking their doing something living in a lie; in other words, not their true self, but one who is trying to live a temporary forever to complete a lifestyle they feel obligated to be.

Meanwhile, not being true to their lifestyle is becoming their reality. The meaning of superficial does not necessarily mean fake, it just means that you live in a fact that is not your own. Maybe a dream you do not put in the effort to make happen. Something that makes you feel like you are doing something, when you are doing nothing but hurting yourself. To be honest within yourself is the first step towards admitting and accepting. To be superficial to someone one pertains to only be interested in maintaining the look or the image.

These people are stubborn and not up for change. So it's either their way or no way. It doesn't mean it's right, or that you have to put up how they process their thoughts. You can gain your control by determining how to handle that person so they do not affect you mentally, physically, or emotionally, and just accept that this is who this person is.

There may or may not be anything that you're able to do about it. You can only change a handful of wandering minds and the other handful, good luck with that. It doesn't mean to give up or that the hope is lost, but you must understand and accept that in some cases, it's a lost cause, and in some, it's just a matter of how much time you feel you want to invest in putting in to resolve it all. We all have those stubborn family members, friends, or even close acquaintances that we encounter, as well as those who we've never even spoken to a day in our lives but who we hear about.

In most cases, you'll know the people you're unable to reach and get through to when it comes to a sense of understanding. Don't let them get you worked up and out of character. I like to say you live and learn, and with the lessons learned comes balance. I honestly believe that there is an unbalance within those types of people, and you need things that grasp their attention or help put them back on track when it comes to losing their way to find a way.

It is about finding and keeping it rather than just making it and overlooking it. The third feeling of self within is your true self. We all know what it means when someone is being true to themselves. It is you that makes you unique. I like to say it is the you that either makes or breaks you once you find out who you are, and the same goes for those around you.

Whether it is something about them or simply about you, once someone understands themselves and the qualities they hold, they begin to find out who is genuinely there for them and who is truly there for their wellbeing. After I discovered my true self, others held the same similarities, but many were different.

Of course, this led to me having only myself to look to and a handful of family and friends. At times people like to believe that family is too good to be true when it comes to envying or someone just not having the best interests, but it can occur within anyone who holds these grudges, no matter how close they are to you. Whether someone is near or does not know you from Adam does not determine one's true self.

First, discover the self within you that allows you to be true to yourself. Second, you must realize who you are, not just who you want to be. Third, find something you are passionate about and not just things you feel are suitable for others' desire, but indeed within yourself that make you happy.

Most importantly, never be hesitant to ask for help to ask for feedback. It is known as constructive criticism, which I feel most people lack the urge to want to hear about. And lastly, one thing that we do not hear about is assessing your relationships. Whether with your mom, dad, brother, sisters, close family friends, grandparents, or even people you touch that may be acquaintances. First, begin by admitting the problems and defining what you would like out of these relationships that you are continuing to hold. Understand the part where it gets touchy, even if that means completely cutting that person's ties.

Understand that not everyone who's a part of your life story is supposed to stay in it. And some that you may come across are only to remain in that chapter. To self-sacrifice plays a massive role in not only those around you but most importantly you.

To self-sacrifice is not a selfish obligation to yourself, but taking the time to understand your worth and self-values, exportation, and overall abilities that you have yet to sit back and absorb.

There are multiple meanings of self-sacrifice in many ways that one can further explain. But which way explains you and how you consider grasping the meaning of self-sacrifice and its relation to you? You have the first example of self-sacrificing and you can use it alongside multiple things, such as putting yourself first before others or even after others..

Are You Willing To Take The Risk

"Self-sacrifice does not always have to be labeled and targeted as something bad. But just know how, when, and why you are self-sacrificing yourself. Along with the multiple reasons of either importance or not so much of importance of something than the next."

-INicole Royce

But who am I to label what you should consider important to one? I give you the ideas and you come up with your conclusions and visual outcomes to overcome self-sacrifice and go in whichever direction you choose. I first will speak on the pros of self-sacrificing.

The pros of self-sacrificing can make a difference and a 360 turnaround for not only yourself, but those around you. I like to say that because this book is about guiding one about themselves; I cannot speak too much about someone else's guidance, but here is how it's suitable for you. When you are working on your own self-sacrificing, that means dropping things or gently pulling away from things that are not leading you in the directions you wish to follow. Unfortunately, sometimes we self-sacrifice the wrong things which lead to the cons of self-sacrificing, such as troubling ourselves. This not only troubles ourselves, but also concerns those around us because of the careless choices and mistakes that we continue to make. We continue to find an out without truly finding an end.

However, learning takes mess-ups and mistakes that will continuously play a considerable part in continued growth. There is a difference between the same mistakes and repetitively followed mistakes.

- **What's growth if you're not gaining from it?**
- **What good is a mistake if you are too stubborn to go into another sense of direction?**
- **How many times have you run into the same wall without switching your direction?**

I would say multiple times, in which I felt like I would never grasp the knowledge needed or the path gained fully. It takes patience and time for someone to understand the meaning behind self-sacrificing completely. In this case, it never has bad intentions; just sometimes we are in the unknown and needed that sense of direction to help us switch our focus. So when I speak on self-sacrificing, I love to guide that positive direction of self-sacrificing, which means following these steps towards getting to know your true self and what makes you the creative being that you are.

What are those things that describe and explain your character and make you stand out more than those situations that keep you in a circle? For example, what makes you place others before you and ahead of you without guiding instead of following? When you find your self-sacrifice, I consider that person to be a leader to be the person who places themselves first in situations they feel that they are just as good enough to be in, instead of good enough to follow in.

Be that person who's good enough to stay in the race and continue to lead and look back and still see themselves with the same amount of power as given when placing others before you on the pedestal you should want for yourself. Having something for yourself has no meaning if you are not projecting it and putting your words into action.

You Are of Importance!

A person can want something all day, but what meaning do your words carry until you put forth the initial effort, the effortless effort? There's a difference between sacrificing yourself and sacrificing for others, and believe it or not, a lot of us feel as if we are doing something right all the time when we put others before ourselves. What good is someone that leads you if you don't feel good enough to follow?

I believe strongly in the meaning of lead by example. So why not want consistency? You are a leader. You should not only want more of others but want the same for yourself. Sometimes we work on others' crafts before fixing ourselves and then have those around us to blame for our faults and misconstrues.

A sacrifice can be a label towards things that hold somewhat of negative empowerment. To sacrifice yourself for something negative is not the only meaning behind the word. However, it is the only way some perceive the word.

When a person performs a self-sacrifice, it means giving up something of desire to you for the more significant within the good of something to help yourself and help others in the process. Not just one person, but a domino effect and continuing. You also have the type of sacrifice that causes things of value to you, and you have to choose which is more concrete than the other, which can be challenging, and there you have "self-sacrificing. "

This is why this is a chapter that I feel everyone needs to meet when it comes to the core and overall values of putting yourself first. To feel the importance of your own acknowledgment as you do for those around you, and find the balance within everything that you come across. No matter how important, remind yourself that if you're not taking care of yourself, what good will someone or something else be?

There's so much that we as people try and take on in what we feel has little to minimum time to prosper. Still, it only takes us longer when we continue to rush and go towards a sense of direction we know is wrong. And sometimes, we knew and were fully aware it's the wrong direction, but we continue to try and knock down that wall when we need to change our path. Things do not always have to be what they seem.

I believe highly in everyone having that same gain of equal opportunities, no matter which route you must take to get there. It might be a little more challenging for some, but with knowledge comes power, and if we all sit and share with the things that we know and the ways that it took to get there and how at times we need to slow it all down, then you'd be fine, but society has you rushed and feeling like you're left behind.

There are so many routes to take, and so many levels that people can go - no matter how long or how much you crumble. There's always room for mistakes as long as one is willing to grow.

I like to share what I learned within myself and those I have met that have guided or misguided me. The situations and circumstances helped motivate me to find a way and believe that putting myself first holds just as much quality as wanting to keep others important too. You have to have a balance, no matter how much you do or how much you're involved, and not like to make excuses for not having the time or not doing something because of your situation.

What good do any of those excuses do for you when making sacrifices that will help those around you and, most importantly, you? It's like something should have just as strong an impact on your sense of thinking and the overall urgency to want better when building your initial growth; another stage to creating you and your personality. Understand change and evolution, and evolve into who you're to become. Not the you that you've been pretending to be, keeping yourself in hiding so that no one can see, but the you that you're capable of being.

If only you take this quality and apply it to yourself as the previous qualities of self, you'll fully understand why this quality stands out. It'll allow you to find that balance.

Have you had that situation you feel you have invested so much in to throw away completely?

Maybe you even try to make sense of things that make no perfect sense. But due to the amount of time spent and the energy given, you feel obligated to keep going. Of course, we all have moments when we feel like this and those times wasted. But you can grow from these, and when you realize you've wasted so much time, you then realize that you're blossoming and have bloomed into a much better you.

To make sacrifices in life seems to be the most challenging. However, some sacrifices are easier than others. But if we knew what sacrifices to make, would things be that hard to overcome? Sometimes, it's only hard because you're in too deep and realize that you've received nothing from it other than a lost cause or what may seem to be a broken heart. Yet, this is all perfectly normal and will lead us to become even stronger individuals as we're destined.

The moment someone genuinely comes around for your best interests, whether it is a mentor, your teacher, your mom, dad, friend, significant other, whoever it is, you will realize the difference. Those losses that were too hard to let go of will become easier to overcome. Once the right situation or person can fill that void, you'll realize that the time and energy are worth much less than your sanity. You'll realize you're digging an even deeper hole for yourself by prolonging unsustainable situations.

I advise you to try something that my mother once told me to do growing up, after realizing that the only person I had to count on was either her, my dad, or my grandparents..

How many people can you stay with that you can help when needed? Whether financially, mentally, physically, or just overall expressing your emotions with? I can truthfully say that my answers are much different now. But she, my mother, told me to look through the contact list of people I called friends and see if they were on of that list. Would I have anyone to call in the case of any given emergency? That was something that I was able to feel. Something that I was able to open my eyes to and realize that self-sacrificing, at the end of the day, no matter how much it hurts, is better.

I realized that when the shoe was on the other foot, what might hurt you would be quickly delivered for the sake of someone else. That is one of the pros of someone having a genuine heart. They do not recognize things for how much it's worth or what they have done but, most importantly, how it makes you feel or makes you think. Truthfully, there's no better feeling than understanding what my mom once made me see as she allowed me to realize that all you truly have is yourself at the end of the day. Letting yourself down should be the only disappointment you have.

When it comes to wanting and needing something, I believe that everyone needs help at a point in time and a helping hand without getting bitten off is of most value. There are many uncertain situations and miscommunications that people feel when it comes to being there for someone. Therefore, before you help someone, I believe it should be genuine. You shouldn't expect anything on demand. Nor should you do something unless you truly have it to give, whether it is for that time or even to help build someone up.

- **How do you help someone build up if you continuously take from them?**
- **How do you expect someone to feel comfortable to ask for help if you continuously throw in their face how much you have done or are doing?**

If you are going to be your person of character, please abide by being your true self. To remain who you are is all the explanation that you need. And when it is all said and done, always maintain yourself and keep those close to you closest.

It would help if you took the time to allow people who want to enter your life to earn that trust and become their natural self. Do not be so quick to open them to what you have to offer, but open them to the sense of mind you have towards thinking. To talk to people nowadays is what I offer before lending a hand, because you do not want to become unworthy of materialistic relationships.

Suppose someone is willing to listen to you and abide by your sense of thinking. Then, you might have a positive route to take alongside a beneficial relationship for both of you. There are so many people out there choosing to be hurt; rather than choosing to do right. Of course, some challenges and consequences follow the two, but of course, how could you blame someone based on what they are going through or have gone through?

It is all about keeping your eyes open and just dedicating yourself to taking a completely different route than once before. From experience within myself, I have learned that my heart is and will always be a giving one, but the awareness I have now for those who enter my life is less than gullible. I don't treat anyone any differently, but I'm a firm speaker when it comes to letting you know where I stand first-hand with things, whether it's how I feel, what I think, or possibly ways to mend things broken in a sense. I never like to leave things on a negative term, but you live, and you learn to choose what battles are worth being fought wisely. Everyone's examples of what they have experienced are somewhat similar, but have a different way of being delivered.

The things you say and the interpretation behind them speak volumes that more people can feel rather than see right away. And once you get too comfortable, you will then be able to match up the words with your actions. Be firm in what you believe in. You should never feel that your opinions do not matter or are less or more important than someone else's.

To be entitled to your sense of thinking is not a crime. Maintain that same level of urgency when it comes to sacrificing something for someone else as you would do for yourself. There's such thing as refining yourself and rebuilding.

No matter how big or small, you feel that one thing could either maintain a huge outcome or an even smaller one, depending on your delivery. So take these words as words of encouragement and try them. Consider finding something different you've either not done before or have been tempted to try but never followed all the way through. I promise you will not regret it.

SELF-SACRIFICE

BEFORE reading the chapter

1. What exactly is self-sacrifice?

_____
_____
_____
_____
_____
_____

2. What does self-sacrifice mean to you?

_____
_____
_____
_____
_____
_____

3. What have you dealt with in life that complies with you having to self-sacrifice whether your experience has been good, bad, or indifferent?

_____
_____
_____
_____
_____
_____

4. How does self-sacrificing make you feel in the process and the long run?

_____

_____

_____

_____

_____

_____

5. How do you feel that self-sacrificing can or has sustained you as a person, whether it's been physically, mentally, spiritually, and or your overall emotional well-being?

_____

_____

_____

_____

_____

_____

AFTER reading the chapter

1. After reading this chapter, does your answer to what self-sacrifice means stay the same or change after reading?

_____

_____

_____

_____

_____

_____

2. After reading this chapter, do you feel as though you now have more control over the way self-sacrificing had possibly made you feel from your past experiences?

_____
_____
_____
_____
_____
_____

3. Below write some words of wisdom that come to mind you after reading this chapter in motivation to yourself.

_____
_____
_____
_____
_____
_____

4. What is something you wish others truly knew about you when it comes to you as a person and your overall personality?

_____
_____
_____
_____
_____
_____

5. Exactly when do you know that enough is enough for you?

_____

_____

_____

_____

_____

_____

CHAPTER 9
SELF-REDEFINING

"You need to clear yourself and create another mental space for your mind to grasp hold of things, and a deeper mind behind the average mind. It is a must that you recreate yourself to become the best in the long run for those around you. There are always eyes watching, and the mind over matter is within yourself and your own. It starts and ends with you."

-INicole Royce

To begin where self-understanding leads. The meaning behind self-refining is to redefine yourself and understand your true value clearly. The ability and capability of awareness when it comes to an understanding of your actions in place of others' reactions to something. I cannot stress enough when I say that something that's understood is sometimes more about understanding someone. As people, we react to situations firsthand instead of allowing ourselves to process the outcome of it all mentally.

- **What good are words when the action doesn't follow or vice versa?**
- **What good are your actions in place of words that are unclear, with unclear meaning because you only have half the answer that you need?**

Meanwhile, you're speaking upon what you've heard instead of what you actually know. And you're coming up with conclusions that could all be consequential at the end if not handled with care. When you understand yourself more clearly, you will then understand the qualities behind self-understanding. You will understand your capabilities for things and will not be putting yourself down.

To see your challenges and to uplift yourself, while recognizing what you have is a gift. You have the overall power within yourself to accomplish the many things you probably felt that you could not, by simply just not giving yourself the proper respect you should. You need to understand that self-redefining comes from someone recognizing their capabilities, character, feelings, and overall motivations that allow them to gain a sense of that extra push needed to push through. This is not saying that you do not need to be you, but that you need to become a better you. To many who change for the better within themselves when it comes to self-redefining, they find that others know that they have changed.

- **What exactly is self-redefining?**
- **Are you self-redefined?**

And if not, how do I or will I go through the? Why is it that when one considers redefining themselves into something, having somebody to help you means you become agreeable to the change that you weren't able to abide within yourself? But you feel as though you're left behind, when that same someone who helped guide you leads themselves to true success. When will we realize that everyone has the same journey and the same truth as anyone else? That nobody is as good as the next, it all takes time and, most importantly, discipline. It is better than who or what someone has, and when you're focused on redefining yourself, the motion changes; it becomes see-through. Speaking from experience, my ideal experience from self-redefining has become purer than anything.

I have allowed myself not only to grow from the many mistakes that I have learned, but I do not have the amount of support that I thought I once had. Now I have more support from myself. It is funny to me because we must have numerous people's attention and become something; we must be recognized by something or for something. We sometimes do not understand what it means to be respected for not what you do, but what you stand for. I was that person who once thought the number of people you knew determined your outcome, and I have never been that person who has been surrounded by many. I have always been my own person but, in some cases, more easily influenced than the next.

Meanwhile, I was knowing what was right while at the same time feeling as though I could extend the truth or see how far I could get; wanting to see where I could be going in the midst of it all. There are multiple reasons for one's actions, and no one will utterly understand the meaning behind how and why you are but you. There is so much ideal reasoning behind something, and it will take a lifetime to figure it out. There are so many people who feel the void of caring but who are careless with themselves.

It is all about knowing the difference and being able to separate those people. When it comes to you properly self-redefining yourself, you have to seek balance. You have to know and understand that those you don't want around will most definitely come around, and they'll come around ten times harder than once before. The moment you have grasped yourself and taken the time to understand your meaning? That is the time where you will be able to face those challenges you weren't able to face because you weren't in the mental position to, and you'll know how to go about them. The challenges you will face will be the same as you have always faced.

To other people who have not been on the same journey, it is like you have changed to them while they have stayed the same. And those who are not genuine are the ones who end up looking along the way because they no longer have that negative energy off you. I believe that energy is most of the reasoning behind what you do and, in most cases, the situations you choose to place yourself in. If you realize when a person's energy is pure, not many people follow genuinely trying to cause harm. But some people do follow, making you feel as if you are doing something wrong when you do all that is right.

You must understand the change that you must go through to get to the success you wish to reach soon. To self-redefine yourself, you have not necessarily to be able

192

but, most importantly, be willing to make a difference in your livelihood. It's factual that your goals and achievements will begin to change and soon become a sneak peek of your reality, instead of a dream. Once a person redefines themselves, it allows them to accept better, understand better, and achieve more than you felt you've have achieved ever in life, all because you let faith lead. If you are not physically, mentally, and emotionally able to self-redefine yourself, then the meaning of life you are living is a waste of time. As harsh as that sounds, it is factual - agree to disagree.

You need to be able to redefine yourself after being defined the day that you lived to experience life on this earth. Be willing to not only expand what you've learned, what you know, and things that you could continue to grow from by gaining knowledge from your peers; those who aren't close to you rather than close at times can be your biggest and best outlet.

Sometimes it is the ones close to you who fail to seek your best interests, and those on the outside who grow fonder of you each day. But what good is it when someone else sees potential that you do not even allow yourself to take full credit for? That's when self-redefining takes its course and change comes along. You have to want better to do better, and you have to have hope to seek attention. You have to seek attention to gain the knowledge you have, to gain knowledge to grow, and be open to overhearing the sound of your voice over one who's where you're trying to be.

A Product of Your Environment

Many of us love to listen to those who are not practicing what they have preached—those who are a product of their environments, whether good, bad, or indifferent. You can't judge what you do not know about, nor can you have an assumption or an input if you're unwilling to abide by the constructive criticism one might deliver upon you and your wrongdoings or faults. To self-redefine could step on a lot of toes and either make or break you in the process of it all.

The main reason behind something this strong is that it starts with you, and how you choose to overcome any situation plays a major key to how it ends with you. All of this could have a huge effect on how one continues with their daily due diligence. When you come to the sense of genuinely wanting to self-redefine, you must be open and willing to do a complete 360 and accept the least expected. Sometimes people need to redefine themselves.

For some, it may just take a little to nothing or some tweaking here and there; not much because of the mind frame he or she might already be in, and that has a lot to do with how you handle certain situations, especially when they're not your average topics of discussion. Those who aren't open and willing to hear what they've never heard of won't change the way they think. They may or may not be open to change, whether it's for the better in themselves or just the environment, and you have to understand there's not only a time but a place for everything. And to be one-sided is never the answer.

Throughout time and mostly through experience and continuing, I've learned that it's now much easier to conquer every situation that I come across because I'm past that stage in my life where I can accept my flaws or feel defeated or attacked when constructive criticism has been brought to me. I have learned how to handle things and deal with many things in life. It doesn't mean that you don't have to have a voice or have your opinion. But understand when, where, and how to go about expressing your opinion properly.

All of this leads to self-redefining. I look at this meaning as something that you must do to grow and adjust yourself and learn manage your feelings.

The way you react and respond to things will not be as easily revoked; the messages you deliver should be signed instead of just delivered with no entitlement. The respect you wish for should be accountable, for what you say is held by you or someone else. It's the respect that paves the way towards your sense of entitlement. Anyone can come out of something out there; we all have flaws, we all have things that we are not proud of and are continuing. We all have situations that don't always have the ending we'd like. But yet, we have always been too prideful to admit or take complete ownership of our wrongdoing.

Whether it's the delivery of how someone may have said something in one way to another, it is a matter of fessing what is wrong and not always just what is right. It is about helping the situation and uplifting one another to fix yourself, while others accept their flaws. The more people point the finger and continue to blame people with weakness they will not feel comfortable redefining themselves, as they most likely feel attacked. I love to open people up.

To help people understand that the only way out is in, and it starts within yourself. You can instill something within someone else easily. We have all given advice and been frustrated in the process, because we have yet to resolve our problems but are always lending way for someone else's. It is very human to be frustrated about something as such, and yes, I too have experienced those feelings. It's not as if you don't wish to be there, whether it's lending an ear or physically helping but in the process. Of course, you're frustrated with your own path and sense of direction, which you feel is taking you backward. The emotions you carry come out because you have no other way to control them without retaliation.

They do this through what you think you are, your silence, or even verbally speaking or posting throughout the media, which has become a trendy outlet for one to subliminally speak volumes about expressing how they feel towards someone or something.

My purpose as a primary example is that most people of today will continue to keep things balled up until they are ready to explode. Then, you are steady, never knowing or understanding the many reasons behind the questions of why. There are so many ways to get through to people, but not many people willing to get through. There are multiple people with a cry as loud as your own, or the perfect amount of silence with the loudest cry ever. It is a matter of tuning in and touching others and yourself when it comes to being connected. As humans, we feel we have a huge sense of entitlement or obligation to something without seeking help or understanding.

Instead, we do what we feel is right at that time. And by the time you know it, you've lost your way. We all have times where we feel a certain way, but try asking yourself these questions - after you have calmed down.

- **Do you feel like you've handled the situation right?**
- **Does it somewhat bother you at the end once you can finally settle down and fully process it?**
- **Have you already decided without thinking, and yet it is too late to go back and change how you have reacted?**

Gaining Self-Control

All of these things take place in the understanding of the meaning behind self-redefining oneself. Until you completely figure out your technique for how to grasp your self-control, you'll continue to be a work in progress until you can move to the next level of completion; once you've done so, every difficult encounter will become even easier to address. I like to let people know that there's always a way out. It may not be how you planned or the thing you thought would lead you in the right direction. But never feel as if you're alone in the process, because you are not alone. It would help if you took a moment to think things through for those who have it down to manage your redefinition. It's never too late, and there is never too much time to take in when it comes to finding and figuring out more ways to better yourself for those around you and vice versa, bettering those around you sometimes for yourself.

There needs to be more of wanting to reach out instead of wanting to keep everything in for yourself, when knowing that you have could easily influenced many others all at the same time. To gain a sense of hope while bettering myself has led me to do the same for those around me continuously. I hope that this chapter is touching many who are second-guessing or completely over hills with their thoughts and need a light shined on their way to lead them back towards the sense of direction they need to be going in. There's no such thing as late. There will always be room for change for anybody who wants it.

If you have a purpose, you have to find it, and sometimes it takes that little urge or reminders from someone to remind someone else of their worth. Never should anyone feel as if they're alone or feel as though nobody's listening, which is why I hope you find something out of this passage. You have all of the questions, not enough answers, and some have all the answers with not enough questions to match. It's a must that you remain true to yourself, redefining yourself within you; it's never a dull moment when dealing with anything to do with building you into becoming a better you. Everyone has their own sense of understanding and what may be simple to you does not always fall so simply to someone else. When you open your eyes and realize that you can abide by yourself and what you stand for, and remain clear of what's going on right in front of you, is when you've succeeded.

I love to say that there are so many ways to let a person down, but many more ways to lift a person. And that we all should try it for a change. There's enough knowledge, empowerment, and leadership to go around, so why not be that within your own circle? Most people feel the need to want power, and power is dangerous when not handled properly. It's within everything you do, everything you say, and most importantly, the actions that are shown in place of it all when there's a firm believer in self -redefining, and how it not only helps you but those around you.

We can be that example that we all wish to be in the eyes of someone else. That amount of energy that we believe or want those around us to believe that things are okay when they're not. Those moments when things look too good to be true in the eyes of those around you. But you know that it is too good to be true, and not the real you. The moment you understand self-redefining, you will notice the change you allow yourself and the change you will show to others. Those who are truly genuine to you will lead by example and follow.

The Objective

The people who are envious will be exposed more than you will ever know. I like to share another example following that statement that I just made. "Those who are truly genuine to you will lead by example and follow. And for those who aren't and who lead to envy, they will be exposed clearer that you'll ever know." The thought of someone envying you and looking up to you are examples within that someone is not redefined. Some people look up to you but envy you, because you're most likely where they want to be or wish to go. They're seeing where you are going in the direction they wish to go. These will be lessons as well as tests, and not every test is bad. It quite fun and challenging in its way. It will help you learn more about others and confirm the direction and steps you want to go in.

Versatile Thinking

You will begin to look at all things differently, and not so upside-down but right side up, realizing and understanding that while thinking you were the abnormal one, that you are the norm. It will be kind of nerve-wracking at first, and throughout time, it will continue to be nerve-wracking; after opening your eyes, you'll feel as though it should be easy for others to open theirs too. Some people's eyes may open, yet you'll have some who will forever remain closed because of their closed-mindedness. They, see no way but their way, and anything different is a negative for them. To develop self-understanding into redefining is tedious but not uncertain. You should try looking at yourself as the objective more than the problem or just the change you want to become, even if you're the person who doesn't want that form of change.

Therefore, I am creating this book to possibly help open you up with all these judgments and misconducts that make it more challenging for you to see within yourself. I believe that everyone should have some writing tool and be writing down your thoughts following your goals, plans, whether it is for that day, your future, or whatever the case may be. Write down your ideas by brainstorming a little outside of that box you have been used to sitting in, not allowing your true self to express itself. Write about that lifestyle you are trying to maintain but struggle to keep up with on a day-to-day basis.

I advise everyone reading this chapter and this book to perform a self-reflection and compare you before and after. Before, you probably had little to none when it came to ideas. And the other half probably had ideas they felt were not good enough to share, but those ideas were worth so much more than sitting in your head. Have you ever stopped to analyze yourself? To see what you like, what you do not like, things that get you worked up, things that you give in on, and things that make you happy?

To see those things that keep you moving forward and going on a day-to-day basis, take the time to realize that you're headed somewhere with the motive to get somewhere and not just for the time being. People like to

say, "I'm just living for the day." It would be best if you
don't just live for the day but the future ahead of you,
ahead of those you touch mentally, physically, and emotionally, those children you bring into the world, whether
biological or, as I'd like to say, a bonus. Everything you
come across has something to do with you and any representation of what I consider to be perfectly perfect examples of self-refinement.

You need to actually understand which challenges
are being challenged; and which are to be handled with
more care than the next. To live for the future that you not
only create, but an afterlife after that life. To not live for
the life that you wish to live in the now, but creating
something that will make the future you brought into this
world not be even more challenging than it already is. To
make those goals and life changes simply easier because,
as we all know, this world is becoming more and more
challenging each day.

There's honestly not a day that goes by that isn't more
influential in creating the foundation that I want for any
child that I bring into this world, and for any child that's
not biologically mine, but that I have the honor of being
the public figure for, as well as people who reach out with
the slightest help needed or even the most. No matter the
case with me, to touch those around me is everything in
the world to me. I love attaching myself to those who feel
uncomfortable but trapped. To be the one who guides instead of misguides is the position I have grown to hold
and continue holding while paving my way.

There are no excuses, yet I feel as though we all make them. We all have all things that we must jump over, some bigger than others, but the same outcome can apply. There are biases and non-biased opinions about situations, and it is up to you to recognize who has to seek that help. Sometimes when you need to talk, you would think the ones most honorable to you are the perfect examples, when sometimes those on the outside hit closer to home. To have the characteristic of not being judgmental or seeming as if you're the one to point the blame of being judges has a huge impact on people's lives - the things they do, say, and stand for - and it starts with you.

It starts with gaining that perfect sense of understanding the power you hold when it comes to the word self-redefining and not playing around with fire. It takes that one person sometimes to change a situation to touch many others, even if they only touched one physically. I never like to blame someone's actions for the amount of ignorance they have about something - whether it's their action of doing what they feel to believe is right, or simply knowing that someone is believing in something that we might sensibly believe isn't right. But we feel as though sometimes we're unable to do anything; like nothing can be done.

There's a different someone out there and enough to touch others' minds; it is just a matter of how and which direction you choose to go. I enjoy reaching out to people on a deeper scale than just things taught on a day-to-day basis, and I like to get within others' minds. I like to turn the simple way of thinking into a much deeper concept. I like those around me to challenge themselves right along with me, as I see myself challenging and changing each day, realizing that not everything needs a reaction. While working in silence, your outcome of something says everything that a person needs to know to determine whether or not they're on the right track towards something. I believe that it's not about getting discouraged, but how we encourage one another. You can believe in something and have power over something without feeling empowered.

You can have power over something with the attention of those around you without them feeling overpowered. Everyone needs that time to open and redefine themselves and learn who they are, because there is so much to take on and not enough leadership. There are not enough people out there who are abiding by the lessons they wish to be heard and taught. You have some who say what they say and expect you to have no questions behind it, meanwhile not even truly knowing what questions to ask properly. That is why, within this book, I write my questions, and I allow you to answer. I allow for your mind to wander just as much as mine, and for you to create those thoughts and creativity build-ups that you have always had but never allowed to prosper. I challenge you to try something new and become observant when it comes to one's thoughts or even the thoughts within yourself. To challenge yourself and take the time to see what you face on a day to day basis that causes you to get out of character or to have that interrupted energy. And all of this will lead to another characteristic within yourself.

To build your self-confidence is to identify yourself as the person you are, whether it be in the now or the person you're becoming. To completely recognize your qualities, feelings, and abilities to do or accept what you're not able to do but realize that there is nothing you can't do. It's just the effort you put into being able to make it all possible. I am a walking example of the self-confidence part, because I'm still learning to gain confidence and build in that which I lack things that people either see in me or that I fail to see within myself. And vice versa, things that I know within myself that people fail to see. And I am learning to accept and understand that although I am not perfect, people are just on their high horses and do not allow themselves to face those challenges. And to meet them is experience.

You'll soon realize the confidence that comes with it; because there's certainty within what you are talking about, and that's what you call discipline. You'll also notice that majority of the time, you'll avoid most conflicts because you'll understand the knowledge behind the argument or even discussions that one chooses to turn into an argumentative moment due to lack of experience, leading to proper understanding. A person can have experience behind something and adequate knowledge.

You don't want to be unable to listen to someone else's opinion – you want to have debate but come to a sense of understanding for why one has such belief in his or her sense of thinking without arguing, and coming to what's known to be a compromise. You need to be mindful and follow the steps towards better. Not everything that you feel needs to be heard or needs to be said.

You need to learn when and where things should take place and have your certainty. I believe all who follow these qualities will see something different within themselves, and wonder why it took so long for them to face the challenges they thought would never come around in the best interest within themselves. But do not think that way; continue to pick your head up and remember that experience comes with time.

Everyone's time is valuable, and it just might not have been your time. But the moment you choose to gain the interest of reading this book may just so happen to be your time. To touch those who have not spoken to anyone. To speak to those who have not even the slightest clue who they are within themselves. . To touch those who are the most stubborn and are eagerly looking for something to complain about.

There are characteristics that I feel one should lead to follow and grasp to know about themselves. Why hold back thoughts and creative-minded experiences that I have faced that helped me which could help another? The coincidences that I speak about have reflected me and I feel could reflect someone else. I am all for uplifting and finding multiple ways out of no way. And I hope this book becomes nothing less than a gain for you, never a loss.

SELF-REDEFINING

BEFORE reading the chapter

1. What exactly does self-defining mean to you?

_____

_____

_____

_____

_____

_____

2. Would you consider yourself as self redefined? You should definitely ask yourself, "Am I self redefined ?" and if NOT, "How do I or will I go through the steps to become of such definition?

_____

_____

_____

_____

_____

_____

3. What's your idea of a perfect day?

_____

_____

_____

_____

_____

4. Name a moment or a couple of moments in your life that you'd never forget that actually made you happy genuinely. And describe them in ways of what made them such unforgettable moments.

_____

_____

_____

_____

_____

_____

5. Make a list of 20 things that make you smile.

_____

_____

_____

_____

_____

_____

AFTER reading this chapter

1. Does the meaning of Self-Redefined mean the same now after physically reading this chapter or has your meaning and understanding become different than once before?

_____

_____

_____

_____

_____

_____

2. After reading this chapter do you now see yourself as someone who is either redefined or in the making of becoming so?

_____

_____

_____

_____

_____

_____

3. Are the ideas you had of the perfect day the same after you've read this chapter than they were before? Now try asking yourself again. What's your idea of a perfect day knowing what you know now with a feeling differently than once before?

_____

_____

_____

_____

_____

_____

4. Do you feel the same as you once felt or has this chapter made you feel after reading this chapter?

_____

_____

_____

_____

_____

_____

5. Are the things that made you smile before reading this chapter still the same or have they changed?

_____

_____

_____

_____

_____

_____

CHAPTER 10
SELF-LOVE

"You must see within you what those around you don't or either see but dare not to accept. The only acceptance of accepting is within your own truth, your self-love. Remember to pull yourself together and never lose sight of what you stand for to know that you have a purpose as well as all of those around you. It's up to you to discover you within your own self-love and claim your purpose."

-INicole Royce

When a person loves themselves, it allows you to make more sufficient decisions for yourself. And overall healthy choices in life and with all that you do, whether it's what you eat, the amount of exercise you give your mind, the self-care of you treating yourself or giving your mind that attention. In perfect definition, speaking volumes of loving yourself. Make sure to speak these volumes into your space of existence.

- **What is self-love?**
- **How do you self-love?**
- **What does it consist of?**
- **Why is it important to self-love?**
- **What happens when self-love does not exist?**
- **How do you overcome self-love if you have**

never experienced it?
- **What is the outcome of one becoming self-loved over any other?**

I believe in self-love, which is extremely sensitive because many of us struggle to feel love within ourselves. Although loving yourself should come easily, at times it's quite challenging. But you should never be placed in a situation where you cannot give yourself the love needed. Self-love means taking the time to know yourself and giving yourself that dedicated opportunity to prosper into an even better you. It is not caring about what someone else has to say, but most of all, what you have to say! Whether it is something normal or different for a change.

- **Do you ever take the time to figure out who you truly are and what you stand for?**
- **Do you know what your gifts are and what you abide by when it comes to you as a person?**

To give yourself self-love, you have to ask yourself questions such as: "What do I like? "What are things that I want?" What makes me happy?" so on and so forth. When you are obligated to give yourself the love needed, you are then taking the step into your wellbeing and happiness. I like to say that when you're certain about what your self-love consists of and the things of your needs, then the feeling of love has something that no one can ever take away from you or even make you feel as if you're not worthy - because the only confirmation needed is yours, in which you'll answer to no one other than yourself.

The developments of self-love fall into the place of knowing what it takes to help build up this characteristic. The following acts of self-love developments take the place of acts such as: Being mindful of things and feelings within yourself to put your words into actions, instead of just speaking into your reality. Abiding by proper self-care within and giving yourself multiple choices to help find and motivate your self-mind. You must have boundaries within certain things, whether it's placing yourself on a schedule, having a set schedule, or even things such as what you allow and what you don't allow when it comes to certain people who come your way. Another development of self-love I would say would be to protect yourself. To be mindful of those around you with both good intentions and bad intentions.

For those around you, you never truly know what their intentions are, but this plays a huge role in keeping you in tune with things, which means not only yourself but also with others.

The moment you can read yourself and your inner instinct, you will tell who is healthy for your lifestyle and who is not. At times it could be those closest to you that choose to envy you when you are growing, as well as trying to knock you even lower than you have already fallen. There are people out there, as we all know, with the intentions to hurt, the intentions to belittle, the intentions to keep one down and make them feel as if the world is only as big as he or she can see. And it is much more to our world than the days that we live in and the things that we see on a day-to-day basis. It is up to you to reach for all eternity and to not let anyone misguide you.

Forgiven But Never Forgotten

The next step to self-love development that I feel to be of importance is to forgive yourself. I say the importance of forgiving others is important, but to forgive yourself just as much is needed indefinitely. Not many of us get through situations without blaming ourselves continuously for why something is happening, has happened, or continues to happen. We all have situations that come about which are not so fortunate. Some situations are worse than others, and then some are just on a constant repeat that reminds us either of the past or just a situation that once was, simply because we haven't changed the routine that guidance that self-love gives. We like to give things the benefit of the doubt at times and gain too much faith in things that we should sometimes just let go of.

Continue to Walk in Your Own Shoes

Have you ever dealt with a situation you felt you should've been done with, but you keep trying to knock down that wall then you realize you're running out of time, when in reality, your destine is your time? You have a goal; you have a plan, and that is why you feel as though you are running out of time. Because you, unlike many others, have an idea of where you want to be and when you are trying to get there. I like to say the first thing to realize that is to admit it. And you're giving your self-love by just showing that amount of self-care, whether you know it or not. If you didn't give yourself the slightest bit of self-love, the thought would never cross your mind of you feeling as though you're running out of time.

Whether you know it or not, that is a step towards self-love, and you overall admit and realize that flaw all on its own. We all do it; we all go through it and have been through it. We all have been through situations that have taken a turn for the best or the worse in some way, shape, or form and wish that we could turn back the hands of time, but that's not always the case. You are a step closer to your peak, so do not hold back any longer feeling like you are in any of this alone. We go through things every day that we wish we could change, things that we never wished even happened, yet how you finish determines your strength - nothing that you do following any decision you have made should you feel regret about, when it comes to bettering yourself and your self-love.

If you don't love yourself for allowing yourself to discover what loving yourself even feels like, then how will you ever truly know how to love someone else or share that genuine self-care within and for the wellbeing of someone else? The person who will end up hurt more will be you, because you will end up putting all of that hurt and blame on your own heart, carrying your sorrow. After all, things didn't go as expected. You have to self-love to understand the qualities that will harm you mentally, physically, and emotionally.

To place yourself in an anxious place of the mind isn't a good feeling. You will begin to feel uplifted once you have gained this superpower of seeing yourself get through what you are going through, and you will love yourself even more—the abundance of self-love will surround you.

To me, self-love is the everlasting meaning of putting you before anything and anyone. Does that necessarily mean that one is selfish by doing that? No, not at all; it means absolutely nothing near or close to that. Self-love means to treat, care for, and abide by your love, peace, and overall happiness before paying mind to others seeking their own peace.

You Live, And You Learn

Once you learn to give yourself the love you either look for or give to someone else, you'll understand and overall appreciate the love that's not only being delivered to you but also by you. You'll then not only seek the love that you've been missing, but realize that you're filling a gap that's previously been filled with the wrong kinds of love and other things. The love that is filling the gap is only good for a season, and then what do you have? Ask yourself, where did the love go? Why did that love go? Was it truly self-love, or was it fulfilling love for the time being, for the moment, a filler not permanent; as I'd like to call it a "temporary forever." The moment you learn what self-love is, you will soon be more appreciative and notice when and when not to accept the certain visuals that self-love interprets to you in your everyday life. Because it comes in different ways, shapes, and forms, and it is up to you to know what is good for you and what's bad, because what seems good isn't always, and what's defined as bad isn't always bad.

When I speak to those around me, I speak in ways that will encourage you to think more outside the box rather than to point the finger at one specific thing. The day that you truly began to love yourself, you will not only feel it, but you will understand it and cherish it. The feeling of loving yourself comes with training; it comes with thought, the urge to want better, seek better, and want more than just what could be given by just anybody and anything - because anyone can present love but is it real love? Is it self-love? And when you have that full-blown self-love, you will never be able to be fooled again. You will always have that third eye on the watch for any tedious intentions or any tricks that might be waiting to be presented to you as a trick in the box. That will not happen when your self-love guard is up, because there will not be anything in the world that amounts to the credibility of love you give yourself. Nobody will ever be able to replace or replenish that energy but you! And when you realize it, when you know it, others will partake and understand what is meant to be understood.

- **How do you self-love within?**
- **Have you ever asked yourself how?**

- ## How do you learn to self-love within?

Of course you do; we all ask ourselves how, why, will I ever get through this - if so, when? I have been that person on the other side of these questions. I have been the person who does not know which way to go or even start. I have always had guidance from the special lady who brought me life and who has given me the best life to live, learn, and choose from, to experience the ups, downs, good, bad, ugly, and indifferent with. But would I blame her for there being bad parts? That is the only way to learn; you must fall, and the rise is NEVER easy. And if it is easy, then you never truly learned from the beginning.

Anything worth striving for is worth working towards; nothing ever should be handed. By any means, it is never deeply appreciated until you must use that same drive and energy to do it yourself, no matter how much guidance you have, no matter how much pressure is applied. I can say deeply that my mother has been a tremendous impact on many of the situations, experiences, and overall growth that I have been able to apply in my everyday life, and I am tremendously thankful.

Have you ever truly asked yourself what self-love consists of and if you have had enough consistency or enough to spare? The consistency of self-love comes with patience. It comes with abundance and overall being in the know of things that are not only happening, have happened, and that are about to happen, but being able to overcome any and every obstacle that may feel the need to try and get in the way of it all. If you ever question whether you have had enough consistency, always remember that consistency comes with time, and nothing happens overnight.

Also you may not always have enough to spare, especially not at the beginning - that falls in place of helping yourself before you can help others. If you think about it, helping others while lacking within yourself will only cause you to lose yourself. In this case, how can you practice what you preach if you've yet to do so? And it gets deeper than that. It is life and the cycle of it in which you choose at the rate you choose. It would be best if you remembered that you have full control.

Why is it important to self-love? It is important to self-love; without love within yourself, you cannot give and show your love for something elsewhere or to someone as clearly as you would like. It's essential to love the importance of you and what you stand for, without just living for each day, whether it's for yourself or most of the time we live for someone else. While we within ourselves are at discomfort and not of peace. Like any other, you tend to make do and cater to those around you, but not place yourself first and on such a high pedestal as you place those around you. It would help if you had all your self-motives in a row, because something so small could have such an impact.

What's an outcome if you are not ready for it? I believe in the phrase, "Nobody truly got you the way that you got you." And that statement within itself is factual.

You have those who seek your best interests; you even have those who will stop, drop, and roll for you if you need it. But no matter what, that will always be something to either hold you accountable in the long run, because eventually help runs its course. How do you overcome self-love if you have never experienced it? To overcome self-love with no experience of it is deep. It's not to say that you'll never understand, but it's behind the meaning of the phrase, "Most hurt people hurt people."

It is hard to attract self-love if you have never experienced it. You are only presenting what you have been presented. It is quite hard for me to speak exactly about how someone is to self-love if they've never experienced it, but it's not hard for me to have witnessed that it is every bit possible. It is all a matter of your mental strength all around. When you are accustomed to holding things in and not speaking on things that are bothering you steadily, you question those continuous what-ifs and mischiefs that have you pondering what was and will be. We all have thoughts about these things, whether you've experienced self-love or not. Still, the uncertainty with anything about you and how you seek yourself to be in others' perception won't be as much of a worry to one who's never experienced self-love.

If someone is continuously knocking you down, instead of uplifting and remaining your open ear at times, then what good are they really doing to your soul? You then ask yourself, what weight are they truly taking off your shoulders?

You want to be who's been knocked down continuously and able to overcome those obstacles.

The outcome of one becoming self-loved over any other is more than explainable. It is the way to feel free and abide by the vibrant genuinely behind the meaning of being free. Everybody has their own definition of free. But my overall meaning of free is not just about being where you want to be at the time you want to be, but free spiritually, physically, and emotionally. It's in tune within yourself and your surroundings, not just the abilities you have at that given moment but the abilities and self-qualities that you carry on an everyday basis.

We as people look for things other than deep within ourselves. We look so far for the things that we're indeed capable of, but while it's sitting right in our face, right on our nose, we do not see it. We go around to people, places, and things to look for it, thinking that the ideal motive is to find somebody to lead us there. It takes you to self-love yourself. Whatever is needed of you to believe the truth within yourself, not allowing yourself to be a filler or misguided under someone else's conduct to good or bad, positive or negative - it takes that level of certainty for the self-love that you've built to carry the weight of your outcome, the true becoming of self-love over another. We need not try and find that self-love within things, objects, or even people.

There seem to be toxic cases when looking for self-love within things around us rather than within ourselves. We look so far for things, when the majority of the time we have the answers right in our face. I want for you, if this is you, to take the time and find yourself. To change whatever you are doing right now, this very moment, from this day to the next. To change the way you live, eat, see things, respond to things, the way that you think, the way your daily routine goes, and so forth. Sometimes the daily routines are things we do because we were already accustomed to them rather than because they're healthy. We lose ourselves trying to maintain this outstanding image when more people struggle with the same sense as you.

I've also been this very person who never self-loved, yet knew how much I was worth and how much credibility I had to share and self-love that I wanted to spread throughout. But I never allowed myself to discover any of that and abide by doing just that as I do now. I can say there is so much more out there to live through and experience.

Never feel like you must do something that you would truly rather say no to for someone else's sake. Learn when compromising becomes more about one person doing more for the other than for themselves. You should ask yourself when the last time you did something new was for you, or even when the last time you did something extraordinary and actually felt as if you could be your honest, true self without feeling as though you're living a lie when you're around no one but yourself.

This trait falls in connection with becoming disconnected, which is a feeling you never want to allow yourself to become complacent with. You are always urging yourself to escape from yourself without dealing with different enigmas. For example, situations often require face to face discussion but you find yourself having an excuse for why not rather than how to. You will then begin to feel like everyone is out to get you, and you won't be able to separate business from personal or personal from just physical, day by day situations.

When you start to feel disconnected, it comes with resentment, defiance, stubbornness; all these characteristics that cause one to get off track and which don't lead to self-love. As you're then feeling those ways over many other emotions, you'll start to feel overwhelmed. It is not what you know but how you go about it. It is how you decide to handle the situations, in the best ways possible. I hope for nothing less than self-love towards every single person who has faults and continuous troubles within this chapter, leaving them nothing less than a new leaf turned and the hands of growth, character, creativity, and many more characteristics. Please do not allow yourself to ever get out of your element of comfort, but at the same time, remember that you must be uncomfortable and experience these days of discomfort to appreciate what is received once it arrives.

You need to continue to reach many with the same headspace that you have and the same potential dreams of getting up and out and doing something about the change they wish to be made. There is so much to be thankful for, and yet mindful of, when it comes to self-love accountability. It is not for me to point the finger or tell you any form of information that I've yet to test for myself. Everything is mutual, and the bonds are beyond me. I like to be a continuous product in my environment and speak by experience. What's information if the one who is sharing it is one-sided? There's a voice loud enough for every single person out there, so trust and believe you don't have to keep quiet all the time, nor do you have to feel the need to scream every time something decides to take an alternate route other than the one chosen by you.

To continue to be amazed by your own way of thinking should be one for the books of self-love! The way you think shows your creativity and, most of all, the value that you hold for yourself. The amount of respect you give yourself dictates the love and respect given when crossing paths with another. Self-value will allow you to envision and interpret the many examples that self-love consists of. You will either be continuously made in the process, or broken by the amount of self-love you choose to give yourself. You must love yourself to motivate yourself. You must want the highest of everything and have the belief that nothing is too good or impossible to be true. You are the key to the life you wish to live.

The beginning of how you start it all has no meaning behind the end result. You can start on the roughest track ever and end with complete power. Although you may not utterly understand the characteristics of why something happens, you set the tone the moment you come in contact with any given situation. It is all about how you go about the situation and the amount of respect you choose to give yourself. The self-love characteristic isn't a common trait, although it should be, and you'd think this would be an easy step but yet it's unfortunate how challenging it is. It's up to you to determine what's worth the time you give and what you could seriously give yourself. Always remember that your happiness is everything you allow for it to be.

Your happiness sometimes faces multiple challenges if that is where your mind sends you to believe. Self-love comes from doing things not only because they're the right things to do, but because they keep the balance. To do something that allows your balance to be maintained is huge. Whether you know it or not, balance is what keeps you sane.

The balance within one allows that person to find what motivated them and is something that allows them never to forget the goals and maintain the energy used to accomplish your utmost success. It would help if you tried leading by example, and you can apply that to any and everything in your life.

SELF-LOVE

BEFORE reading the chapter:

1. What exactly does self-love mean to you?

_____
_____
_____
_____
_____
_____

2. How do your self-love? And what does it consist of?

_____
_____
_____
_____
_____
_____

3. What happens when at that moment in time, you feel like self-love does not exist? And how does it reflect on you?

_____
_____
_____
_____
_____
_____

4. How does one overcome self-love if never experienced? If that someone so happens to be you, then how would you respond?

_____

_____

_____

_____

_____

_____

5. What is the outcome of one becoming self loved over any other?

_____

_____

_____

_____

_____

_____

AFTER reading the chapter

1. After reading the chapter on self-love, do your thoughts from before match up to your current response?

_____

_____

_____

_____

_____

_____

2. Does self-love consist of the same qualities that you include them to be or qualities you secluded before reading this chapter?

_____

_____

_____

_____

_____

_____

3. Talk about a moment when you felt like self-love did NOT exist in your reality and how it gained a major effect on you that has either been sealed or still hindering you until this day?

_____

_____

_____

_____

_____

_____

4. After rearing this chapter, do you feel a sense of relief in embitterment towards what is expected of self-love vs. the self-love that you thought you received or did NOT receive at all?

_____

_____

_____

_____

_____

_____

5. How would you share with someone you're ideal thought for overcoming self-love to someone who's never experienced it from your standpoint whether the self-love you received was positive or negative?

_____
_____
_____
_____
_____
_____

www.ingramcontent.com/pod-product-compliance
Lightning Source LLC
Chambersburg PA
CBHW071319120626
46546CB00002B/379